ON COMMUNITY

BOSTON UNIVERSITY STUDIES IN PHILOSOPHY AND RELIGION

General Editor: Leroy S. Rouner

Volume Twelve

On Community

Edited by
Leroy S. Rouner

UNIVERSITY OF NOTRE DAME PRESS
Notre Dame, Indiana

Library of Congress Cataloging-in-Publication Data

On community / edited by Leroy S. Rouner.
      p.   cm. — (Boston University studies in phi-
losophy and religion ; v. 12)
    Lectures delivered at the Boston University Institute
for Philosophy and Religion in 1990.
    Includes indexes.
    ISBN 0-268-01507-4
    1. Fellowship — Religious aspects.   2. Community
life.   3. Postmodernism — Religious aspects.
I. Rouner, Leroy S.   II. Series.
B.50.O52   1991
307'.01 — dc20   91-50285
                                        CIP

For Huston Smith

His Institute lectures have regularly broken new ground. In his fearless challenge of the common wisdom he has been clear, imaginative, and wise. He and his work have made the forgotten truths of the perennial philosophy effective bearers of relevance and new meaning for our time.

Contents

PART III: THE FUTURE OF COMMUNITY

Preface

Boston University Studies in Philosophy and Religion is a joint project of the Boston University Institute for Philosophy and Religion and the University of Notre Dame Press. The essays in each annual volume are edited from the previous year's lecture program of the Boston University Institute. The Director of the Institute, who is also the Editor of these Studies, chooses a theme and invites participants to lecture at Boston University in the course of the academic year. The Editor then selects and edits the essays to be included in the volume. In preparation is Volume 13, *On Selfhood.*

The Boston University Institute for Philosophy and Religion was begun informally in 1970 under the leadership of Professor Peter Bertocci of the Department of Philosophy, with the cooperation of Dean Walter Muelder of the School of Theology, Professor James Purvis, Chair of the Department of Religion, and Professor Marx Wartofsky, Chair of the Department of Philosophy. Professor Bertocci was concerned to institutionalize one of the most creative features of Boston Personalism, its interdisciplinary approach to fundamental issues of human life. When Professor Leroy S. Rouner became Director in 1975, and the Institute became a formal Center of the Boston University Graduate School, every effort was made to continue that vision of an ecumenical and interdisciplinary forum.

Within the University the Institute is committed to open interchange on fundamental issues in philosophy and religious study which transcend the narrow specializations of academic curricula. We seek to counter those trends in higher education which emphasize technical expertise in a "multi-versity," and gradually transform undergraduate liberal arts education into preprofessional training.

Our programs are open to the general public, and are regularly broadcast on WBUR-FM, Boston University's National Public Radio affiliate. Outside the University we seek to recover the
public tradition of philosophical discourse which was a lively part
of American intellectual life in the early years of this century before the professionalization of both philosophy and religious reflection made these two disciplines topics virtually unavailable even
to an educated public. We note, for example, that much of William James's work was presented originally as public lectures, and
we are grateful to James's present-day successors for the significant public papers which we have been honored to publish. This
commitment to a public tradition in American intellectual life has
important stylistic implications. At a time when too much academic writing is incomprehensible, or irrelevant, or both, our goal
is to present readable essays by acknowledged authorities on critical human issues.

Acknowledgments

These volumes are made possible by our individual authors, and our primary debt is to them. The Institute is honored by their willingness to participate in our program, and I am grateful to each of them for the care with which they have prepared their individual papers.

Copy editing and manuscript preparation is done each year by Dr. Barbara Darling-Smith, Assistant to the Director of the Institute. In the course of a dozen volumes her skills have grown to the point where she is now a legend in her own time. Once again Syd Smith has given her valuable assistance, as has James P. Bailey.

Editor Ann Rice at the University of Notre Dame Press sees the manuscript through the publication process with professional calm and good humor in the face of the inevitable crises.

Jim Langford, Director of the University of Notre Dame Press, is our publisher and an invaluable colleague. He has not only helped in our long-range planning, but has participated as a lecturer in one of our programs. His friendship and professional help continue to be one of the Institute's major resources.

Contributors

ELIOT DEUTSCH received his Ph.D. from Columbia University and is now Professor of Philosophy at the University of Hawaii. He succeeded Charles Moore, and served until recently as Editor of *Philosophy East and West*. He continues in an editorial capacity for a number of scholarly publications including the *Journal of Chinese Philosophy* and the *Journal of Buddhist Philosophy*. He is the author of many articles and books including, most recently, *Personhood, Creativity and Freedom* and *Interpreting Across Boundaries: New Essays in Comparative Philosophy* (edited with Gerald Larson).

R. W. HEPBURN was educated at the University of Aberdeen and has taught philosophy at the University of Edinburgh since 1964. A moral philosopher with a wide range of philosophical concerns, he has published many books and articles in the fields of philosophy, theology, literature, and art. Among these are *Christianity and Paradox: Critical Studies in Twentieth Century Theology* and *'Wonder' and Other Essays: Eight Studies in Aesthetics and Neighboring Fields*.

PATRICK J. HILL has been Vice President and Provost at The Evergreen State College in Olympia, Washington, where he still teaches. A pioneer in educational reform, he is the Founder and former Chair of the "Federated Learning Communities," an innovative interdisciplinary program which seeks to address problems of incoherence in traditional college curricula. He is a recognized expert on the role of community in higher education. He has published *Varieties of Liberal Education* and has a work in progress, *The Communal Dimension*.

CATHERINE KELLER studied for the B.A. at the University of Heidelberg and took her Ph.D. at the Claremont Graduate School. She is currently Associate Professor of Constructive Theology at the Theological School, Drew University. Much of her scholarly work has explored Christian theology from a feminist point of view. Among her many publications is her most recent book *From a Broken Web: Separation, Sexism, and Self.*

JÜRGEN MOLTMANN is Professor of Systematic Theology at the University of Tübingen. He also teaches at the Candler School of Theology, Emory University. A member of the Faith and Order Commission of the World Council of Churches and the Department of Theology of the World Alliance of Reformed Churches, he is considered by many to be "the pastor's theologian." Among his many books are *The Theology of Hope, The Crucified God, The Church in the Power of the Spirit, The Future of Creation, On Human Dignity, The Trinity and the Kingdom, God in Creation,* and *Creating a Just Future.*

KATHERINE PLATT received her Ph.D. in anthropology from the London School of Economics and Political Science after field work in the Kerkennah Islands off the coast of North Africa. She is currently Assistant Professor in Social Sciences in the Boston University College of Basic Studies and Research Associate at the Center for Middle Eastern Studies at Harvard University. The author of numerous scholarly papers, she is currently doing research on Tunisian Muslim and Jewish communities in France and Israel.

HILARY PUTNAM is the Walter Beverly Pearson Professor of Modern Mathematics and Mathematical Logic at Harvard University. He has recently delivered the Carus Lectures, the Immanuel Kant Lectures at the University of Munich, and the Kant Lectures at Stanford University. His many books include *Philosophy of Logic; Philosophical Papers* (in three volumes); *Meaning and the Moral Sciences; Reason, Truth and History;*

The Many Faces of Realism; and *Representation of Reality.*
He was a recent participant in the Sixth East West Philosophers Conference at the University of Hawaii.

LEROY S. ROUNER is Professor of Philosophy, Religion, and Philosophical Theology and Director of the Institute for Philosophy and Religion at Boston University. He is General Editor
of Boston University Studies in Philosophy and Religion and
has also edited *The Wisdom of Ernest Hocking* (with John
Howie) and *Corporations and the Common Good* (with Robert Dickie). He is the author of *Within Human Experience;
The Long Way Home (a memoir)*; and, most recently, *To Be
at Home: Christianity, Civil Religion and World Community.*

GEORGE RUPP is President of Rice University. He came to Rice
from Harvard University, where he was John Lord O'Brian
Professor of Divinity and Dean of the Divinity School. He
has degrees from Princeton (A.B.), Yale (B.D.), and Harvard
(Ph.D.) and has also studied and done research at the Universities of Munich and Tübingen in Germany and Peradeniya
in Sri Lanka. He is the author of numerous articles and four
books, including *Commitment and Community*, published
in 1989.

BENJAMIN SCHWARTZ received his B.A., M.A., and Ph.D. from
Harvard University, where he has been the Leroy B. Williams
Professor of History and Political Science since 1975. He is
the former Director of the Fairbank Center for East Asian
Research at Harvard and has also served as the Director for
the Project on the Political Order in East Asia. He has received a Guggenheim Fellowship, and has taught at Balliol
College, Oxford, and the Truman Institute of the Hebrew University, Jerusalem. He has also served as a Distinguished
Scholar in the People's Republic of China. He is the author
of many publications, including four books: *The World of
Thought in Ancient China; Communism and China: Ideology
in Flux; In Search of Wealth and Power: Yen Fu and the West;*
and *Chinese Communism and the Rise of Mao.*

HUSTON SMITH is Thomas J. Watson Professor of Religion and
   Distinguished Adjunct Professor of Philosophy Emeritus at
   Syracuse University. His teaching career has been devoted to
   bridging intellectual divisions: between East and West, between science and the humanities, and between the formal
   education of the classroom and informal education via films
   and television. He is the author of many articles and books
   including *The Religions of Man, The Purposes of Higher Education, The Search for America, Forgotten Truth, Beyond the
   Post-Modern Mind,* and (with David Griffin) *Primordial Truth
   and Post-Modern Theology.* He has also produced television
   programs for the Public Broadcasting System; films on Hinduism, Tibetan Buddhism, and Sufism; and a phonograph
   record, "The Music of Tibet."

MERRY I. WHITE received her A.B., A.M., and Ph.D. from Harvard University and is now Associate Professor of Sociology
   at Boston University. She has worked as a free-lance journal-
   ist, publishing articles in the *Atlantic,* the *Boston Globe,* and
   the *Christian Science Monitor.* More recently she has focused
   her writings on cultural and educational interchange between
   Japan and the United States. She has also served as a consultant for the PBS program "Learning in America" and as a
   panel member on a binational satellite PBS television program, "Face to Face," on Japanese and American education.
   Among her many publications are *The Japanese Overseas;
   The Japanese Educational Challenge: A Commitment to Children;* and *Human Conditions: The Cultural Basis for Educational Development* (with Robert Levine).

Introduction

LEROY S. ROUNER

COMMUNITY MEANS DIFFERENT THINGS to different people. For monks and nuns it means a close-knit, spiritually disciplined way of living the religious life "in community." For people in India and much of southeast Asia it means caste, as when they speak of "our community." And in politics it is often used to summon up hope for a new world order in which there will be a peaceful "world community."

For most of us, however, community is something we don't yet have in the way we want to have it; something lacking which we feel we need. So community is a good thing. We distinguish it from communalism, which is a bad thing because it is either repressive or exclusive or both. Community, for most of us, means some sort of common identity in which we can maintain our personal freedom even while feeling at home with one another.

So in the '60s young people formed communes in California to find community; and today "support groups" of all sorts, from Alcoholics Anonymous to jogging clubs, present themselves as dealing with a problem or an interest, but their most important function is probably providing people with a sense of community.

Philosophically, community is a key issue for what is often called the "postmodern mind." Modernity was roughly that cultural period in the West from Descartes to the First World War when autonomy and individuality were fundamental values in science, religion, economy, government, and the arts. Empiricism in science was a new attentiveness to the behavior of individual entities. Protestantism in religion was a celebration of the individual's relation to God. The rise of the guilds, and the capitalism which followed, was a new form of economic individualism. The *Magna Charta* and the democracy which succeeded it was a cele-

1

bration of political individualism. And in the arts the rise of the
novel celebrated the autonomous life of the individual.

After World War I, however, the autonomous freedom which
attended this individualism suddenly seemed dangerous. More than
that, the loneliness which attended this individualism finally seemed
more than we could bear. Our nostalgia for premodern times when
natural bonds to kith and kin were unshakable had already re-
surfaced, sometimes in dangerous ways. The Aryanism of Nazi Germany was racial communalism at its worst, and it was very powerful. More benign and poignant were the later California hippie
communes, but the same forces were at work, and they, too, ex-
emplified this longing for community.

The attraction of like for like and the fear of the stranger are
surely basic laws of cultural physics. We want to be with our own
kind. We want to find a spiritual place, perhaps even a geographic
place, where we belong. The restless mobility of modernity has
become disorienting and frightening. We want to go home. But
what would it be like to be at home in our world?

No one can yet be sure, but it is none too early to reflect on
this crucial issue, and that is the purpose of the essays which follow. They are divided into three sections. The first deals with Philosophies of Community, and the emphasis here is on metaphysical
analysis and definition of the nature of community. The second
section follows our usual practice of putting our theme in a cross-
cultural context. The four essays in this section are illustrative of
various ways in which community is understood and experienced
in Japan, North Africa, China, and India. Our final section deals
with the future of community and includes essays by both philosophers and theologians on community building in Western societies.

We begin with Eliot Deutsch's essay on "Community as Ritual
Participation." He is persuaded that a person is an achievement
rather than some sort of given; that true community is necessary
for fulfilled personhood; and that this fulfillment comes especially
through acts of ritual and ceremonial participation in the life of
the community. And he is particularly concerned with appropriate uses and potential misuses of power in relation to these ritual
and ceremonial acts. Deutsch distinguishes between coercive power
and creative power. Coercive power is ego-based since it seeks to
bend another to one's own will. Creative power, on the other hand,

expresses freedom and aims to promote fulfillment and harmony. It is authoritative as opposed to authoritarian, since it does not seek coercive domination. It seeks agreement, chosen by those who are persuaded of its authenticity and freely participate in those acts which naturally flow from it.

Deutsch also distinguishes between community and society. Society is a given, "something that everyone is born into and is nurtured by through education and culture," whereas a community is a voluntary venture, "something created by persons within various societies." He describes his position as "creative anarchy" because the culture of the true community is entirely uncoercive and, therefore, the free work of autonomous individuals.

The key value in Deutsch's schema is nonegocentricity. Whereas most anarchists stress individual ego satisfaction as the fruit of freedom, Deutsch argues the opposite view: that genuine freedom leads to a personality which is quietly confident, and fully sensitive to others, but not egocentric in the petty and aggressive ways associated with that term. And the community which results from creative anarchism will not be hierarchical, with an unequal distribution of power. The loyalty which creates community for such a nonegocentric anarchy comes from common commitment to the ritualizing activity in which the creativity of each individual is fulfilled.

Deutsch has suggested that a fairly radical kind of individualism may not be antithetical to community if it is nonegocentric. Ronald Hepburn takes up this same theme in his essay on "Values of Art and Values of Community." Here the issue is the dispassionate, free, autonomous, contemplative posture of attention to the aesthetic world celebrated by Kant and Schopenhauer and Schiller. Hepburn presents their view briefly and then proceeds to defend it against various criticisms. The values he celebrates are "an awareness of freedom, autonomy, of a contemplative posture of attention, in place of a rapacious one, disinterested in contrast to self-interested and acquisitive, in which respect for other beings plays a vital part, and in which there is the thought of a community of sharers in an intelligible, reasonable response to objects of art or of nature."

Hepburn and Deutsch are clearly thinking along the same lines. Community brings together autonomous individuals who

have freely chosen a common set of values and goals. They have
not been coerced; they have come together naturally. In opposition to this view, however, is the contention that social and historical influences make it impossible for there to be any genuine
individual autonomy. Hepburn finds historical determinism self-
defeating, pointing out that the presenter of the argument requires
freedom from such determinism in order to make the argument
valid. Hepburn claims this same freedom for himself.

In arguing for a community standard of reasonableness in
evaluating a work of art Hepburn appeals to the common-sense
view that some art is good and some bad; that the community needs
some standard for distinguishing the good from the bad; and that
a reasonable standard is the only universal standard available. But
autonomous reason requires transcendental resources in his view.
Hepburn relates his aesthetic theory to religion, arguing that dispassionate appreciation of the work of art also requires "a center
of stillness, an origin for its ordering perspective which is not itself in the field of stimuli," and is essentially a religious perception
of transcendence.

Hilary Putnam's paper analyzes Wittgenstein's "Three Lectures on Religious Belief." The relation of his analysis to the problem of community is indirect but significant. In Hepburn's defense
of a religiously grounded autonomous rationality he noted that
opponents of his position would not accept his argument. One is
left with two different views unable to be "in community" with
one another, not simply because they lack common ground, but
because their opposing logical structures are incompatible. Putnam's thesis is that Wittgenstein's analysis of religious language
breaks down many of the logical structures of interpretation which
have kept religious people and nonreligious people from understanding one another. The result is not a theory of religious language but a critique of such theories. "In short, Wittgenstein is
telling you what *isn't* the way to understand religious language.
The way to understand religious language *isn't* to try to apply some
metaphysical classification of possible forms of discourse."

For example, nonreligious philosophers have often used the
problem of reference to discredit God-talk, on the grounds that
God was not a clear object of reference. Wittgenstein counters that
this is not helpful since religious language is both like and unlike

ordinary language, and that "referring" to God for the religious person is quite unlike "referring" to an object of immediate empirical experience. Wittgenstein's position on religious language is therefore both open and respectful of views which he himself does not necessarily share. This is an intellectual attitude which any genuine community requires. Wittgenstein's negative critique clears away barriers to the kind of creative community making which both Deutsch and Hepburn propose.

My own paper on Ernest Hocking's metaphysics reflects on the work of an American philosopher for whom the issue of community was central. In his doctoral dissertation he worked out a theory of the relation among the three fundamental objects of human experience: the self, other selves, and physical nature. He integrated this metaphysical study into his philosophy of religion in *The Meaning of God in Human Experience*, which was notable both for its dialectical structure and its application of that structure to practical religious life. Toward the end of his life he wrote *The Coming World Civilization*, which argued that Christianity could be a community-shaping force in the postmodern world.

Much of my paper deals with the details of Hocking's dialectic, focusing especially on the view that natural objects are the necessary content of mind, and that we share a common mind with others through our common perception of these natural objects. Hocking's interests were wide, and he never completed the statement of his metaphysics which he outlined in his Gifford Lectures on "Fact and Destiny." I conclude, however, with an evaluation of his intention "to defend the realism of physical nature as both fact and idea; that selves are both individuals and inextricably bound in community; that even God is both Whole and unfinished." This metaphysic is a qualified dualism and therefore not entirely congenial to the qualified nondualism which informs Deutsch's creative anarchy. However, Hocking stands with Deutsch and Hepburn in defending both the individuality of the self and the self's communal nature.

With these metaphysical reflections in hand we turn to historical community life in various world cultures, beginning with Merry White's discussion of "Global Japan: Internationalism in the Intimate Community." White begins with the surprising statement that "Japan's number one *domestic* issue today is interna-

tionalization." Her point is that "Japaneseness" is a very important value for contemporary Japanese society, and that Japan's
growing role in the world community threatens that distinctive
national culture, especially in the lives of those Japanese who have
occasion to live abroad for any extensive period of time. White
details the inherent conflict between the "new Japaneseness" which
is an international identity, and the cultural uniqueness which
makes most Japanese see themselves as distinct from other national
communities.

White explores this issue through a focus on the intimacy of
Japanese life, especially in the home. She notes that the Japanese
word for intimacy is the same character that is used for *parent*
and that the dependency of children on parents is encouraged.
There is little tension or opposition within the family. As a result,
family life is cohesive and nurturing. Children who have lived
overseas, however, return to Japan from a different cultural atmosphere and are regarded as having broken the tight bond of
the cultural group. White notes that intimacy has many values,
but that it tends to promote conformity and lacks the strong autonomous individuality which Western philosophers like Deutsch,
Hepburn, and Hocking find essential for community. It is clear,
however, that there is nothing in Western life comparable to the
homogeneity of the intimate Japanese community, and White concludes with the hope that a modernizing Japan may be able to
maintain "the support and solace" of these communities in the
midst of modernization.

Katherine Platt introduces a new dimension of community
making with her focus on geography. For our previous authors
community has been established socially through individuals participating in ventures involving common rituals and common values. Platt is also interested in this process, but she is especially
interested in its geographical setting. Her essay deals with "Ritual
and the Symbolic Geography of Community," and the specific setting is Tunisia and the Kerkennah Islands just off the coast. The
islands are home to many who migrate for various periods of time
to Tunisia or even to Europe. Platt analyzes the ritual of return
to the homeland and the function which this geographic place plays
in the community identification of its people. Her thesis is that
"one's identity as a man, a woman, and a Muslim of good reputa-

tion and right practice is established and renewed through a series of life cycle rituals and annual Islamic holidays. In order to be effective, these rituals must take place in a social field void of anonymity and which is a complete moral universe. . . . The place of origin reliably provides such a context. . . ."

Platt argues that ritual return to the geographic place of origin has economic significance as well as therapeutic value, since, for example, the trade union movement in Tunisia is dominated by Kerkennis, and the ritual return to Kerkennah validating one's community identity is also an employment qualification in Tunisia. And in religious practice, this particular place functions as a *means* to being a good Muslim. "Kerkennis do see their islands, not as a sacred place but rather as an austere guide to a proper Islamic life, similar to the rule of the Qur'an." Platt's essay thus provides specific illustration of the thesis she shares with Deutsch concerning the significance of ritual in community making.

From Platt's specific study of a local community in North Africa we move to Benjamin Schwartz's more broadly gauged study of the concept of community in Chinese culture. He begins with a review of recent sociological reflection, especially the distinction between individualism and Ferdinand Tönnies's notions of "community" (*Gemeinschaft*) and "society" (*Gesellschaft*). He also notes Emile Durkheim's argument for the significance of religion in community life.

Turning to China he acknowledges that one is struck by the "overwhelming presence of the social in all its forms" but he makes three observations which temper that generalization. One is that this socialization does not carry the ontic weight in China which it has had in the West. A second is that "in many ways individuals play a role of supreme importance in traditional Chinese high culture and even in the popular culture." And finally, China did not experience the radical disjunction between the cosmic and human realms which is so characteristic of the post-Cartesian West.

Schwartz is at pains to point out the distinctions between Chinese "individualism" and the individualism of the West, especially noting that Chinese individualism does not lead to human rights grounded in law, the "economic man," or the individualism of aesthetic romanticism. What he does argue, however, is that the idea of the community in China, because it does not have a great deal of ontic weight, "depends on the moral quality of its constitutive members." This delicate balance between individualism and community has a good deal in common with the spirit of Deutsch's creative anarchy, and is clearly different from the collectivism of the Marxist-Leninist regime in contemporary China. Schwartz concludes wryly, "The opposition view that the emperor may be wearing no clothes is much more in keeping with some of the main tendencies of traditional thought."

Huston Smith takes us in a different direction. His essay on "Dignity in Difference: Organic Realism and the Quest for Community" is more metaphysical than the other essays in this section, and might well have found a home in our first section on philosophies of community. I have included it here, however, because it takes the Hindu notion of caste as a paradigm, and suggests a sympathetic second look at social realism. Western views of community tend toward idealistic models. In America, for example, no truth is more sacred than the affirmation that all are created equal. As it stands, of course, this is simply not true. It is a prospective value for us, based in notions of human dignity, and made effective in equal treatment before the law. The dirty little secret of Western equality, however, is that in most of our lives we have a hierarchy of values which ranks social worth. It is better to be president of a university than janitor in a university dormitory. Smith does not challenge the prospective value of this egalitarianism. He is concerned, rather, with the simple fact that different people have different gifts and capacities. And he asks how we might recognize this difference within the context of equal dignity.

Taking time and space as standard measures, his question concerns the size of the world which different people occupy. He suggests that there is a type of person whose world does not reach much beyond the realm of the senses. A second type expands to include family and friends. A third type includes the entire planet. A fourth type sheds all boundaries, extending to the infinite. He concludes that his characterology is negotiable, but "what I cannot get away from, and hence am not prepared to back down on, is my sense that society is organic." Its organs, he argues, are distinct human temperaments. He insists that this kind of social realism can help carry us toward a just and true community.

Our final section on the future of community begins with

Patrick Hill's paper on "Religion and the Quest for Community," which deals with the relationships among religions and how those relationships might be rethought. He sees two sets of values in conflict. The first are values associated with modernity and democracy, such as freedom, self-determination, individuality, and diversity. The other set of values are those embodied in premodern and preindustrial societies, such as loyalty, rootedness, solidarity, responsibility, and civic pride. He advocates respect for the inevitable diversity arising from this conflict and suggests several dimensions of that respect. One is to value diversity as part of community, and not assume that what is common is inherently more valuable than what is diverse. Another concerns "the ecology of community," especially understanding how communities both grow and decay, and establishing criteria for evaluating communities. A third is to value diversity so that one does not conflate understanding of another tradition with assimilation of that tradition.

Regarding the role of religion and the integration of various religious communities, Hill continually emphasizes the positive role of diversity. He criticizes those who look to another religion only to claim in it what is similar to one's own tradition. "What is missing in interreligious dialogue . . . is a sense of inadequacy or partiality, a sense of genuine need of the diverse other in order to accomplish some desired objective." Hill's idea of community is one in which "differences have their home, and nonmanipulative and reciprocal interaction is possible."

Jürgen Moltmann has done a number of theological essays for the Institute, but here he turns to philosophy for an examination of the relation between "Knowing and Community." He states the issue directly at the outset. "Knowing and community are mutually related to one another: in order to come together in community, we must know each other; and in order to know one another, we must come into contact with each other and enter into a relationship with one another." He argues that the theory of knowledge and the laws of sociology are thus inextricably intertwined, and his paper sets out to analyze this connection. He begins with Aristotle's affirmation in the *Metaphysics* that "Like is known only by like." His paper is a critique of this Aristotelian principle. Like Hill he wishes to celebrate difference, although for him this is ul-

timately the difference between ourselves and God. He proposes
parallel principles from the theory of knowledge and from sociology. The first is that "Different is known only by different"; the
second is that "Community in diversity makes life interesting."

Moltmann also agrees with Hill that the interesting thing
about the other person is the ways in which that person differs
from me, not the ways in which we are similar. He applies this
in his conclusion to our knowledge of God. "Dialectical thinking
says that God appears as God in the realm of that which is different from God, that is, in the realm of humans; dialectical thinking says that for humans God is totally other." Some have argued
that the otherness of God makes God unknowable to humans, but
Moltmann's argument is that only in otherness can God be truly
known.

Catherine Keller's intriguing title is "The Apocalypse of Community." Her point is illustrated by the people of Israel in exile,
giving birth to the genre of apocalypse as a means of maintaining
their beleaguered community. But her concern is focused on the
development of patriarchal society by the Hebrews, and its failure to take note of the oppression of women in their midst. A major theme of her essay is suggested in her comment that "a feminist perspective discloses not only the patriarchy of apocalypse,
but the apocalypse of patriarchy." Apocalypse clearly has both
negative and positive connotations, and she later develops a positive feminist connotation for a positive apocalypse which will break
the mold of patriarchy with an emphasis on futurity, community,
and earthiness.

Keller sums up her view by arguing that "community is a
cherished, chosen expanse of interrelation, in which relation itself
is examined, maximized, nurtured, stretched; in which 'loyalty'
toward 'the common good' is pursued; in which interrelationship
becomes praxis." The apocalypse of this kind of community is a
threat which she hopes can be avoided, and she urges "patience,
not grandiosity; attention, not dualism; earth, not escape."

We conclude with George Rupp's essay on "Communities of
Collaboration: Shared Commitments/Common Tasks." As his title
implies, his argument is that there can be no community without shared commitments and common tasks. He is less concerned
with the aesthetics of community, as in Deutsch's reflections on

ritual, and more absorbed in the problem of work. He notes that even in the traditional communities of Asia, where bonds of blood and soil were once major community-making forces, the challenge to traditional ties is evident. He notes that national communities like India are caught between the religious traditionalism of the past and the secular modernism of its present. In such a situation the future of whatever community may mean in India is in the balance.

Rupp's vision of the future of community is realistically focused on our central activities, including especially our work. Even here, however, in the erosion of the earlier notion of work as vocation to the present view of work as an occupation, the community-shaping power of common tasks has been eroded. Rupp argues that "the challenge we face is to extend the contexts in which this sense of community through collaboration is attained." Further, "insofar as our work exemplifies such collaboration, it may provide a sense not only of individual identity but also of participation in community that is the more crucial insofar as a society is dominated by impersonal markets and bureaucracies."

Our authors represent diverse interests but they also share common ground. Virtually all are agreed that a creative community needs some form of individualism in order to make a community effective. And there is common agreement that community is a good thing and that the quest for community in our time is a significant cultural fact. Surprisingly enough, there is little reference to ways in which community can become communalistic and therefore totalitarian and oppressive, so our authors also share a common ground of hope.

Finally, the critique of the liberal view of the autonomous individual which has been so strong in recent years, and in recent volumes in this series, now seems muted. This is perhaps a good time then to turn to the nature of the self which makes community possible. With that issue in mind, the next volume in this series, *On Selfhood*, is now in preparation.

PART I

Philosophies of Community

1

Community as
Ritual Participation

ELIOT DEUTSCH

A PERSON, I BELIEVE, is an achievement, not a given. A human being is a person to the degree to which she or he becomes an integrated, creative, freely acting, social, and moral being. A person
is thus a bearer of dignity—and affirms quite spontaneously and
naturally the intrinsic worth, the dignity, of every other human
being and, insofar as possible, of every other living thing. How
then, one need ask, does a realized person conduct himself or herself politically within the matrix of social relations and community? How, in short, ought a person to be with others?

I shall subscribe here to what I will call a "creative anarchist"
position. I will outline this position by way of a brief discussion
of the general concepts of *ritual/ceremonial action*, of *power*, and
of *nondominance* in interpersonal relations. I will then develop
these concepts in the context of *community* and will argue that
a community is rightly established by way of the ritual participation of persons acting in the spirit of "creative anarchism."

I

Let us begin with ritual/ceremonial action. We often distinguish in our daily conduct many different forms of action: practical tasks, occupational work, leisure activities, and so on. I want
to talk about ritual/ceremonial action not so much as a kind of
action but as a style or manner of acting that can be present, in

15

varying degrees, in all forms of action. Although the ceremonial and the ritual, as I will show, are often distinguished, I bring the two together under a joint category as they so often intertwine and overlap and, especially in our social relations, happily combine into an integrated style.

A ritual, it is usually thought, is a rule-bound act which seeks, through the exercise of some kind of inherent power, to realize an end that is extrinsic to the act itself (from bringing rain to maintaining, as in early Vedic thought, the entire universe). Rituals are repetitive in principle; indeed, according to many historians of religion, a ritual is more a reenactment of an event than just another event itself. Rituals, in short, answer to archetypal, cosmic, or ontologically grounded happenings. Rituals thus require to be performed correctly, their efficacy lying precisely in their being in accord with various "rules" or principles of being.

A ceremony, on the other hand, is usually conceived as a socially defined action, with the emphasis on regulative rather than constitutive rules, which essentially marks various turning points in a person's life (confirmation, graduation), commemorates past events (birthdays), and the like. Ceremonies are often performative in character (weddings) and, although conforming to certain patterns and structures, are inherently particular. *Rightness* rather than *correctness* as such becomes the criterion for their successful performance; which is to say, the uniqueness of the particular ceremonial action is recognized and the attendant specific features of the occasion (including the special qualities of the participants) are necessarily brought into play. No two weddings are (and no one would want them to be) exactly alike.

Ceremonies, of course, do often have a presumed ontological grounding, which is expressed not so much in a power sense but in the context of their appropriate space/time occurrence. In highly ceremonial cultures like the traditional Chinese (India being the land of ritual *par excellence*), the right time to perform various ceremonies and the right place for them to be performed is of the utmost importance.

The common features of ritual and ceremonial action do, however, for our purpose, allow us to bring them together. The ritual/ceremonial is inherently communal in character and is sustained by tradition. An orthopraxy becomes its rule, so that more often than not the answer to why one does a particular ceremonial/ritual act is, "That is the way it is done."

So far we have been speaking of rituals and ceremonies as kinds of actions, which is indeed the typical way in which they are discussed. I have said that the ritual/ceremonial can better be seen as a style of acting rather than as kinds of acts, and it is to this that I shall now turn. The ritual/ceremonial as a style or manner of acting embodies, I think, a special attitude of participants, an attitude which is precisely that of *participation;* the ritual/ceremonial actor becomes part and parcel of the creative process which brings the act into being. It is his or her willingness to share actively in the event — to turn oneself over, as it were, to the action — that contributes to the special power that is then realized in the act. When acting in a ritual/ceremonial manner, then, the purpose of the act and the reason for it coincide in the sense that any justification for the act would specify the purpose of it. Actions that are performed in the ritual/ceremonial style, in other words, have no justification apart from what is realized intrinsically in their performance. This will be of some considerable importance when we develop this whole idea of the ritual/ceremonial in the context of our interpersonal relations and our community with one another.

II

Let us turn now to the idea of *power*, to which I have already alluded. It seems that all of us need, and therefore oftentimes desperately seek, to be able to effect change, to control others and ourselves, to influence events, to acquire some degree of mastery over our lives; in short, to have power. Power takes many forms — from a crude display of physical force exercised against another, to a spontaneous expression of authoritative competency, such as is exhibited by a master artist. There are raw physical acts of violence; there are subtle manipulations of others; there are legitimated modes of compulsion; and there are triumphant self-overcomings and acts of beauty and grace.

We need then to distinguish broadly at least between coercive power and creative power. Coercive power demands the obedience of the other (be it person, event, situation) to one's own will. It is ego-based. It assumes struggle, engagement, victory, or defeat. Creative power, on the other hand, seeks the realization of a harmony that is constituted in and through diverse and oftentimes otherwise conflicting elements. Creative power is an expression of freedom in action. It is exercised in celebration and in joy.

Creative power is thus not, as it has often been thought, an imposition of some kind of rational order upon chaos, a therapeutic overcoming of the forces of darkness, or a simple overflow of exuberant feeling which is expressive of its bearer's personality. Rather, it is just that mastery, that skillful acting, which is grounded in an essential understanding of things and of being, and is realized concretely in consummate forms of acting freely. Creative power, as we have said, unlike coercive power, aims to promote fulfillment and harmony in particular situations. It translates into the political/social arena as the authority which issues from competency: the *authoritative* in sharp contrast to the *authoritarian*. Creative political power, as I will try to show, strives — while seeking to attain its own proper ends — to enhance the dignity of persons.

III

Persons, we have said, are social beings. An isolated, totally solitary person would be a contradiction in terms. A person sees another person, however, not just as necessary to oneself, but as that other person may be part of a relationship that enhances human dignity. A person doesn't seek to dominate another person, albeit individuals as such indeed oftentimes do. Throughout the realm of social relations, nondominance, as a positive, creative attitude or style, is the political stance of a mature person.

Nondominance is thus essentially the translation of creative power into the politics of social relations. It is both a training in self-cultivation, in the achievement of personhood, and the fruit of that training. The more one is a person the more natural it is for one to act with and toward others nondominantly. Without effort, one extends oneself to the other, man or woman.

The exercise of nondominance nevertheless has perhaps its harshest challenge in the relationships between men and women.

As feminists have so ably taught us, in almost all societies, for whatever reasons, there has been an assumption of male superiority, and a corresponding exploitation of women, with much of that tacitly accepted by many women.

Nietzsche has Zarathustra urge a man to bring his whip when encountering a woman. "Thou goest to woman? Remember thy whip!" And he remarks in *Beyond Good and Evil* that

> men have so far treated women like birds who have strayed to them from some height: as something more refined and vulnerable, wilder, stranger, sweeter, and more soulful — but as something one has to lock up lest it fly away. (237a)
>
> To go wrong on the fundamental problem of "man and woman," to deny the abysmal antagonism between them and the necessity of an eternally hostile tension, to dream perhaps of equal rights, equal education, equal claims and obligations — that is the typical sign of shallowness. . . . (238)

But why this evil, this need for subjugation which deprives the oppressed and the oppressor of the fullness of their personhood? The psychologist in us will assuredly answer, "fear." But fear of what? Is it because women make evident men's own helplessness in the face of all the radical contingencies of life? Is it because, as some feminist writers would have it, men, having been compelled historically to reject and repress much of their own gentle and sympathetic nature, project that "femininity" onto women in order to keep it at a distance? It might even be argued that nondominance is itself merely a soft, feminine ideal which is best left to women, that men need a more robust idea of striving and triumphing which will produce strength and fortitude.

The answer to this, of course, is that there is nothing weak or submissive in nondominance; on the contrary, it exhibits the greatest strength and self-confidence and lies within the capability of all persons, male or female.

Persons, grounded in the conditions of individuality, are sexual beings — and are so, as Freud and others have convincingly shown, from early childhood to the waning years of old age. Sexuality is at once body-based, as an organic drive, an energy, a force, and psychically constituted as a need for enhancement, intimacy, recognition. It clearly assumes different meanings and is

expressed with varying intensities during the different stages (biological and social) of one's life, for both men and women. And
as Foucault has demonstrated, sexuality has a history in its diverse
cultural manifestations and representations.

Let us call the sexuality that is a given of one's biological nature (albeit as always socialized through various cultural forms)
"primitive sexuality"—primitive in virtue of its originary or primal
status. Primitive sexuality is the raw physical drive for release and
completion; the basic source of attraction (and repulsion); the
energy, the libido, that excites and yields pleasure of a uniquely
poignant intensity. Everyone knows, because everyone enjoys or
suffers, this primitive sexuality; few know what to do with it; many
allow it to assume degrading or what we might call "fallen" forms.

Fallen sexuality is a kind of moral madness, a turning of oneself over to the body in such a way as to focus every strain of re-
sentment and rage through it and upon another who is then reduced to that same body. Fallen sexuality is the pornographic, the
hateful and violent. It is a deprivation of human dignity.

The sexual life of most persons is, however, happily carried
out in more "democratic" frameworks which accord equal rights
to the partners and which call for the negotiating of various needs
and wants with some degree of mutuality established. The ideal
"liberal" form is that of the sexual being a natural extension of
an abiding love between two persons which sustains their intimacy
as well as, when appropriate, allowing for procreation. It is a moral
domesticating, as it were, of the primitive; a respectable eroticism
which allows the sexual to retain something of its original nature
while bringing it into the structure of care and concern.

Historically we have as well the religious ascetic — the passionate *bhakta*, the devout medieval mistress of the Lord, the bearer
of *agape cum eros* — who sublimates primitive sexuality, redirecting its energy toward a divine being, with the hope that the sexual
may be conquered so that the spirit can realize itself completely
apart from the body. The celibate ascetic is, however, engaged in
what appears to many of us to be a hopeless struggle, for he requires the very energy derived from the sexual in order to overcome it. Being obsessed with the temptations of the flesh, she is
only plunged ever deeper into its power.

There is, though, a mode of sexuality, a style of being sexual, which is certainly not fallen and goes considerably beyond liberal mutuality and traditional religiously grounded ascetic renunciation. It is a sexuality based on ritual play, a style that we associate with the creative anarchistic manner of nondominance.

As ritualized, sex means the *participation* of the partners in a spirit of devout offering — not so much to each other as such but to and within a spiritual power that is itself made manifest in and through the ritual activity. The *Bhagavad Gita*, a sacred text of Hinduism, proclaims that all actions should be performed in a spirit of *niskama karma* — acting without attachment to the fruit of one's actions; acting with devotion, with skill and mastery, in the knowledge that all actions finally represent nature and a divine will acting through one. Sex then becomes a genuine *performance*, which is to say, it becomes an acting out of the raw energy of the sexual, giving it both aesthetic form and transformative meaning. Ritualized sex thus requires that the participants turn themselves over to the union, each giving to it a concentrated, disciplined, non-egocentric attentiveness. Ritualized, playful sexuality retains to the full the raw power of the primitive while transforming it into a spiritual achievement. Sexuality here becomes ecstatic in virtue of its transcending quality. It is a way of acting freely in a creative togetherness which generates, like all ritual activity, the very conditions for its fulfillment.

IV

Social relations are not, of course, carried out only in the more intimate or close relationships between individual human beings. There is also the larger social setting, the *society* in which persons live and to which they bear continuing political relations.

We need, then, when extending the politics of social relations into the larger social setting, to distinguish sharply an anarchist ideal of *community* from the reality of *society*. Social relations no doubt occur within both forms or structures, but whereas a society is something that everyone is born into and is nurtured by through education and culture, a community is something that is created by persons within various societies. An individual is necessarily a part of some society or other; a person participates in a community. A society, then, is a preexistent impersonal structure of socioeconomic, cultural relations of which a person is simply a part in virtue of his or her historical being in the world. A community, on the other hand, comes into being in virtue of the voluntary participation of its members. For the individual, a society is a given; a community is an achievement. The creative anarchist is concerned to transform as far as possible the actuality of societies into the ideality of communities.

We have said that persons *participate* in communities. Participation, as we have seen with the sexual, is involved in ritual. It requires a certain openness and sensitivity on the part of the participant, a willingness to contribute to the evoking of a special atmosphere or presence which becomes the basis for further personal involvement. Participation is thus not so much a relationship between an individual and a group, as it is a mode of being together with others in such a way that something entirely new is engendered. A relationship implies the preexistence of that which is related; participation gives rise to that in which one participates. There is thus a kind of communion present in all genuine community: a coming together in an attitude of celebrative harmony.

There is thus an aesthetic, a form-giving dimension to community, for participation means a sensing of what is right and appropriate for the given situation. A wholeness is created which tends then, like a work of art, to have a life of its own. A community, further like a work of art, expresses that quality of freedom which we associate with self-determination.

Community, however, connotes more than a transient encounter between persons, no matter how intense that encounter might be. *Community* suggests something enduring for a considerable period of time; it suggests a tradition. Communities need not, to be sure, extend over many generations, as perhaps full-bodied traditions require; in any event there is a traditional dimension to a community that gives it what appears to be a life of its own. Although a community is only in virtue of the participation of its members, it nevertheless endures in a way that allows it to accommodate new involvements and to accept old resignations. A community thus becomes the ongoing repository, as it were, of the participation of those who have constituted and who presently constitute it.

It is important to note, however, in this context that participation in a community does not mean that a person loses herself in a group, or simply turns himself over to another. There is a fundamental difference between a community and a cult. A cult tends to reduce persons to their bare individuality, with the relationships they bear to each other, and especially to the leader, diminishing their humanity. A community is constituted by autonomous persons, each of whom is enhanced as a person in virtue of his or her participation.

There is, of course, always the risk that a community will degenerate into a cult, especially if there are strong personalities involved, and this points up the further risk in communitarian participation that the openness and sensitivity that is called for does make the participant vulnerable. But there is a peculiarity in this vulnerability, this exposure of personhood, which is that real openness, as distinct from superficial good fellowship, comes from a strength of spirit, that special nonegocentricity which transcends potentially destructive egotism.

By nonegocentricity we do not mean the utter annihilation of the ego. We mean rather the attainment of that spiritual indifference which shows a person as having a quiet confidence, a firm self-assurance, and which allows him or her to be fully sensitive to the other. Nonegocentricity is characteristic of the person who is free. When one acts out of integrated personhood, unselfconsciously one is involved in one's activity. The little *I* is simply not there to be destroyed.

Returning to the ritual character of communitarian participation, there is one further feature which links up closely with these questions of risk and vulnerability, and that is once again *power*. In community there is power — not the coercive power of dominance, but the creative power which we associate with freedom. A person's actions are free to the degree to which they are masterful and are carried out in a certain spirit of devotion and concern. Freedom thereby becomes a quality of the action itself, with the actor enjoying as well as engendering a power of concentrated being. So in community — where persons freely participate — a power or presence is brought forth and is experienced as an inherent quality of the community. It is a power that is there for-itself; the participants partake of it as well as engender it. Being for-itself, communitarian power binds participants in deep and informed feeling.

A community is thus similar in many ways to a family. A family may be, and ought always to aspire to be, a community. A family, though, does tend to become more like a cult than a community because of the unequal roles of its members and the need, at various stages of a child's growth, for some kind of authoritarian leadership, no matter how benevolent the intent. For an individual, his or her family is something like a society. She finds herself a part of it and is expected to fulfill various functions within it. He is dependent upon it for the satisfaction of basic material and emotional needs.

A community in the creative anarchist mode, on the other hand, is not, and can never properly be, hierarchical in the political sense of an unequal distribution of power. Just as those who participate in an elaborate ritual will contribute to the performance in different degrees, so participants in a community will be involved in varying ways; but no involvement is coercive and each involvement is accorded full respect.

Where there is community, then, the style of those who are in positions of leadership is one of orchestrating the necessary involvements of others in order to advance the welfare and dignity of all concerned. Where there is community to the full, participants act spontaneously in accord with others in imaginative ways to satisfy common needs and realize common purposes.

What then, it might be asked, is the common interest or cement which, apart from common ends to be attained, holds a community together? Members of a society are held together by their recognition and acceptance of the fact that their membership is necessary for their survival and growth; participants in a community by their loyalty to it.

By *loyalty* I do not mean blind, uncritical support. The demand for this kind of loyalty calls for the deprivation of the loyalist's being. It is an insulting claim to make upon another that she should support me even if she believes that what I am doing is wrong or possibly injurious to another. This is servitude, not loyalty as a creative anarchist wants to understand it in a communitarian context.

Loyalty is a noncalculating, open-ended offer to contribute

of oneself whatever is required to sustain that presence of belonging-together which is the community. Participants in a community undertake this kind of tacit commitment. They will be loyal to the community because they place a special value upon it and are willing to give of their being to it. Loyalty is a "serving" of oneself as an act of love.

When, as persons who are free, we participate with love in a community we give rise to those very conditions which allow personhood to be fulfilled. The fact that a community is an achievement, not a given, does not imply that it is something artificial, that it is in some way unnatural. Quite the opposite: there is nothing more natural than that persons should strive to achieve community, for in that achievement there is an enduring enrichment of their being. Communitarian loyalty is part and parcel of men and women as political/social beings.

To sum up: I have tried to outline what I have called a creative anarchist position regarding community, seeing the latter as it involves a ritualized participation of its members. I use the term *creative anarchist* to distinguish this position from most forms of traditional philosophical anarchism, which has understood itself as an alternative anthropology and political theory and which has served as a standing critique of all existing forms of government. The creative anarchism advocated here certainly has some connections with traditional anarchist thought, of both an individualistic and collectivist sort, namely, with its aversion to coercive power and its emphasis upon voluntary association and compact and cooperation instead of competition. But it differs from that thought in a number of essential ways. Creative anarchism is not, first of all, a revolutionary political program; it does not seek the overthrow of democratic institutions in favor of some kind of proletarian rule, for it understands anarchism as a style of action which can be carried out effectively only by persons as such, whether worker or professor, male or female, rich or poor, and not by mass action. Second, creative anarchism does not call for the abolition of government; it asks only that the ideals which it announces serve as the standard for all political/social relations; that these relations be informed by the concern to enhance dignity through the exercise of creative power.

It is this creative power which is exhibited so nicely in all genuine community. It is, I have argued, a power for-itself, which is to say, its value is intrinsic. A community, unlike a society, is for its own sake and is recognized as such by its participants. The actions of its participants are thus ritualized in the sense that they express precisely a devotion that is grounded in spirit, that they exhibit care and concern, an aesthetic form-giving content which seeks to promote an abiding harmony. Community as ritual participation thus becomes one of the highest expressions of human freedom.

2

Values of Art and
Values of Community

R. W. HEPBURN

I

CHALLENGED ON THE RELATION between the values of art and the values of human community, a substantial number of writers on aesthetics would present a story on roughly the following lines. To appraise the relevance of the aesthetic to moral and political life we do not have to look at specifically didactic art but to pervasive, perhaps necessary, features of *any* art appreciation, and of aesthetic attitudes to nature as well. We can focus, they would say, on certain capacities and postures of the mind, crucial to the aesthetic, but with a vital bearing on the moral sphere also. From Kant we take the idea of aesthetic freedom, the aesthetic as a "free play" of faculties disengaged from their normal conceptualizing, cognitive roles. We come to "a sense of our freedom from the law of association." Poetry, for instance, "expands the mind by giving freedom to the imagination. . . ." "Imagination . . . is a powerful agent for creating . . . a second nature out of the material supplied to it by actual nature." More broadly,

> the beautiful is the symbol of the morally good . . . and only in this light . . . does it give us pleasure, with an attendant claim to the agreement of everyone else, whereupon the mind becomes conscious of a certain ennoblement and elevation above mere sensibility to pleasure from impressions of sense.

The aesthetic is an area not of passivity, but one in which active, autonomous reason has strong hold. Individual judgment is not "subjected to a heteronomy of laws of experience . . . [but, in this domain] it gives the law to itself, just as reason does in respect to the faculty of desire."[1]

The "disinterestedness" or disengagement central to Kant's account of the aesthetic is developed and dramatized in Schopenhauer. For Schopenhauer, aesthetic experience is temporary release from normal, causal, manipulative, often brutal engagement with nature, and from its anxieties and threats. It is contemplative, rapt. Friedrich Schiller would also feature in the story. For him, "It is the aesthetic mode of the psyche which first gives rise to freedom." "Beauty is . . . the work of free contemplation." And all the themes I have so far mentioned are present in Schiller's *Letters on the Aesthetic Education of Man* (1794–95):

> From being a slave of nature . . . man becomes its lawgiver from the moment he begins to think it. [What hitherto] dominated him as force, now stands before his eyes an object . . . [with] no power over him. . . . Spirit cannot be injured by anything except that which robs it of its freedom, and man gives evidence of his freedom precisely by giving form to that which is formless. Only where sheer mass, ponderous and inchoate, holds sway, its murky contours shifting within uncertain boundaries, can fear find its seat: man is more than a match for any of nature's terrors, once he knows how to give it form and convert it into an object of his contemplation.[2]

It is the merest reminder, but it will have to do: a story of the awakening, evoking, stabilizing — through aesthetic experience — of an awareness of freedom, autonomy, of a contemplative posture of attention, in place of a rapacious one, disinterested in contrast to self-interested and acquisitive, in which respect for other beings plays a vital part, and in which there is the thought of a community of sharers in an intelligible, reasonable response to objects of art or of nature. Freedom, respect, reason; on this account even without direct didacticism the bearing of the aesthetic on the moral and the general life of community is clear. It is not *just* that "the beautiful is the symbol of the morally good"; but the aesthetic perspective as such is symbolic of morality.

No doubt these same conceptual materials, together with an

"expression theory" of artistic creation, already in Kant, could lead to an intensely individualistic and "Romantic" picture of the artist, withdrawn from the community rather than participating in its life. They do not, however, *necessitate* such a picture. Among the actual Romantics, after all, some of the greatest were extremely active in the moral and political scene of their day.

We do not have to leave those same clusters of ideas in the aesthetic writings of Kant and Schiller to find bridges from aesthetic to *religious* values and attitudes. What, for instance, Kant called "aesthetic ideas" can be sensuous embodiments in art of "rational ideas" which elude or transcend any full realization in experience, but to which art may "approximate." Such ideas include those of God and the divine creation of the world. In a somewhat different way, Kant's analysis of the "sublime" provides another aesthetic-religious bridge. For this is experience, at once daunting and exhilarating, of magnitudes or energies too great for imagination to grasp. In this we have an analogue in aesthetic experience, of "numinous experience," which in Otto's classical account is also two-fold, daunting (*tremendum*) and gripping (*fascinans*).

At certain points in the *Letters*, Schiller too builds aesthetic-religious bridges. I shall quote a striking example at the end of this essay.

Impressive though it may be, this "standard" post-Kantian story today meets strong philosophical criticism. I want to outline some aspects of that criticism, and to attempt a response to it. I believe that the positions I have outlined contain too much truth — and important truth — to allow them to be jostled out of our grasp in the crowded forum of current debate. *Both* for what they say about aesthetic attitudes and experience *and* for their implications for key values of community, they are worth more defense than they have recently been enjoying.

First of all, the initial Kantian account is held to be seriously one-sided, and to underestimate the importance of social and historical factors within the aesthetic itself. It sees aesthetic activity as essentially self-emancipation from the given, whether the given of nature or of society, so fostering a sense of individual freedom, together with respect for other being and the reasonableness that works for critical consensus. It understands aesthetic vision as the peeling off of concepts and determinations of all kinds,

as we work back to the ideal of a pure and free contemplation —
with innocent eyes. In fact, it is argued, we cannot have innocent eyes; society conditions the way we see. Even the basic aesthetic attitude itself is not the product of free individual reflection; on the contrary, it is the "product of the entire history of the
field." "Art," wrote David Novitz, "does not merely exist in society,
but takes its character from that society." Nicholas Wolsterstorff
writes of the "need to take account of the social embeddedness
of art."[3]

There are aspects of these counterclaims which are undeniably true, and which my initial "standard" account has to be able
to reckon with if it is to survive. Other aspects are more disputable. We have to acknowledge, for example, that even the most
creative poet works in a medium that is already a social artifact;
a musician may work within an idiom where his or her listeners
have already come to have habits of expectation — of what counts
as a cadence, what dissonances one may or may not leave unre-
solved. And these are more deeply interiorized than are mere codes
or conventions. Painters, be they rebels, satirists, or conservatives,
lean on a tradition that shows through in their painting — whether
to be negated, mocked, or gently reworked.

Some would want us to go further and see art as such as a
"social practice"— or set of social practices, developing their own
self-tuned standards, tasks, and criteria of success — all internal to
the practice, the "game." That such developments occur within
the arts cannot of course be denied. We *could* go further still,
to the institutional theory of art. This theory suggests that it is
not the delighted and sustained contemplation of the individual
spectator, nor indeed the anguished creative struggles of the artist, that constitute the authority for the judgment, "This is a work
of art!" It is rather the art world, variously constituted by different theorists, that confers that status; and objects do not and cannot have it until the art world pronounces. In that theory, I think,
we have one sort of exaggeration — the taking to an *il*logical conclusion of a mode of thinking with sound and important things
to say, short of that extreme point.

Another way to exaggerate is to move from the tenable position that traditions, idioms, artistic problems have their *histories*,
to the very different position that this history is to be understood

deterministically, and as bypassing the freedom of individuals. That yields a view which clearly nullifies our first standard picture, which was precisely an account of the awakening, sensitizing, of individual freedom and autonomy through the aesthetic, through the arts, and instigating a relation with objects and persons that promised a freely conferred respect for other being.

Let us consider, then, how far our Kantian-Schillerian position on aesthetic and moral values could take account of these challenges and threats, or whether they have made it untenable, as some contemporary theorists allege.

First of all, the institutional theory of art: A defender of my "standard" view would want to argue that there is no necessity for the individual to abrogate aesthetic judgment in favor of the verdicts of the art world, however constituted. Any of its conferrals or denyings of art status to particular works and styles of work can be subject to individual reappraisal, by the art world's own criteria, or by other criteria, in the light of the individual's grasp of the history of art and of the human needs and wishes that art works can serve. If the act of reappraising automatically sets a person within the art world, then the concept of *art world* has been expanded to the point of vacuity, and we can elide it away.

Are we to think of the art world as having its own criteria — any criteria — for its verdicts? If it has criteria, then there can be no good reason for excluding anyone at all from reflecting in terms of these, and indeed from challenging the criteria. The fence round the art world can be pulled down. But if it does *not* apply criteria in coming to its verdicts, then that is to say these verdicts are arbitrary and ill founded, not verdicts to which we have any good reason to defer.[4]

The theory certainly poses a threat to the concept of individual autonomy and to the open and free art-critical dialogue vital to my post-Kantian account. We do not betray the Kantian view in respecting some judgments about art more than others: the art historian's, the critic's, the artist's. But we commit a version of the naturalistic fallacy in *totally* deferring to any expert group or restricted establishment. In the *ethical* sphere, if we put great weight in determining our duties on the actual form of ethical life in which we have our being, the network of relationships which is seen as generating moral claims and rights, we nevertheless cannot rule out the possibility of appraising that form of life itself in its entirety, and finding it morally unacceptable. So too in the aesthetic sphere, we cannot rule out using our individual aesthetic judgment to appeal against any art world verdict on a candidate for the status "work of art." We may manifest our autonomy, in either case, in being alienated from the established verdicts and forms of life. But to find oneself so alienated is not in itself to have one's ethical or aesthetic judgments invalidated.

We might put this more strongly. Knowing something of the nonaesthetic, commercial interests involved in the promotion and the selling of art works, and the dangers of confusing aesthetic and nonaesthetic factors, we have serious reason to keep reaffirming the ultimate aesthetic autonomy of the individual and the importance of her or his participation in critical dialogue.

It would be a pity, however, to establish a polarization between the individuality of the autonomous aesthetic subject and the concerns of collectivity, whether seen as the art experts or as society in general. Nor do I have to abandon the Kant-Schiller account in order to avoid such polarization. In a study entitled *Kant and Fine Art*, Selim Kemal explores very specifically the links in Kant's philosophy between fine art and culture. I shall quote a few sentences from near the end of that book.

> Without denying the autonomy of fine art — its satisfaction of aesthetic criteria — Kant . . . [reveals] an intimate relation of individual to community and nature. Here solidarity with a community does not imply that an individual is absorbed and lost in some larger whole. Kant's insistence on individual autonomy in aesthetic practice and judgment affirms the social and political value of subjectivity, imagination, and creativity. Fine art and the experience of beauty contribute to changing the consciousness and motivations of people; and people, in turn, can change the world.
>
> [Kemal writes of the] ways in which [the] *aesthetic* has participated in the struggle to wrench human freedom from natural necessity and from the corruption of an irrational domination of individuals by each other or by social and natural forces. . . . We would need to recognize and understand . . . the relation between individuals fostered by the creation

and appreciation of objects using [the different aesthetic media].[5]

Even though Kemal may in his book have overstressed this side of Kant's thinking in reaction to commentators who have ignored it, an impressive general view emerges, of highest relevance to my theme.

So we seek to clarify and defend a view of the autonomy of aesthetic judgment, and the autonomy of the creation of art. We need a view that consents neither, on the one hand, to the obliterating of individual freedom in the verdicts of aesthetically privileged groups, nor to the diffused social determining of the aesthetically fashionable or what is alleged to be aesthetically available and unavailable. Nor should this view, on the other hand, affirm an unlimited or absolute freedom — which would arbitrarily fail to heed the dense historical, social, and cultural context in which new art is fashioned and earlier art reappraised. I find help in this, in the literary context, from T. S. Eliot's seminal and still relevant essay, "Tradition and the Individual Talent" (1919). Writers — artists in any medium — are initially aware of the tradition in which they situate themselves as a body of interconnected work daunting in its seeming completeness. The task nevertheless is to add to that corpus, despite its completeness, so that the new work both patently reckons with the tradition and leaves the tradition modified and, as a different totality, again complete. Even the radically innovative may be mapped in similar terms. Compare Ian Ground, in a recent book on aesthetics:

> to insist on the importance of the idea of a medium within which are embedded traditions, rules, maxims . . . is not to deny that people may work against the grain of tradition and history or may produce art in relative isolation from the traditions of the medium. On the contrary, we need this notion to explain how there can be a grain against which an artist may set himself.[6]

In the context of philosophy, secondly, we need a view of freedom that draws on, and modifies, themes in Hegel and in F. H. Bradley. It is in a "form of life," a tradition, a set of practices, that our freedom is largely "objectified" and our very identity largely founded. But provision has to be made for that freedom and that sought-after sense of identity to express themselves also in transcending the given social, moral, or aesthetic practices through criticism, dissidence, and creative reform. There we have the essential pattern: full acknowledgment of the social practices, the traditions, the "games" that are played, but a refusal to abrogate the role of potential individual critic, or creator, in either sphere.

Alternatively, we could think here in terms of a duality between freedom and respect. On the one side, we do see ourselves as wrenching human freedom from natural necessity and from other forms of domination including past art, but on the other side avoiding a lurch to the opposite extremes, such as contemptuous dismissal of all past art and its traditions.

Have I in all this been aligning myself with the altogether reactionary? Not at all dogmatically so. But let me illustrate. Writing of five artists of the 1980s (Hiller, Beuys, Cahn, Gormley, and Hodgkin), Sandy Nairne comments:

> They make arresting images which acknowledge, but are not dependent on, previous uses of the same material. They make imaginative transformations of material, . . . imaginatively extending what sort of worker the artist might be.[7]

About Carlo Maria Mariani, whose work looks back to the painting of the late eighteenth and early nineteenth centuries, Nairne comments: "The traditions of painting are such that emulation and reworking have long and distinguished histories. The continuity of painting as a practice partly arises from the fact that certain subjects and ideas recur." Jorg Immendorff, he says, "sees the past as a component in the present which has to be struggled with"; and he reports Anselm Kiefer as saying, "History is a material to be used like colour, as part of a complex mix of materials, references, and associations that fill his paintings."[8]

I should want to add, more broadly, that good art scholarship and sensitive writing of art history can enhance aesthetic freedom through enhancing the grasp of live creative options revealed by extrapolating lines of development from the past. Striking instances, one of which I shall elaborate a little later, include the persistence through transformations of Romantic vision, across markedly different idioms down to the present day, and the expression, in undogmatic painterly terms, of a sense of the religious-transcendent. But, conversely, if art history is crudely done, perhaps simplistically ordered to suit an ideological imperative, the outcome will instead be an impoverishing of freedom, a cramped sense of present possibility.

Opponents of the view I have reworked from Kant's, Schiller's, and Schopenhauer's materials are unlikely to be appeased by any of this and may present a more thoroughgoing challenge on the following lines. The disinterestedness, contemplativeness, disengagement, which I would understand as the conclusion of a process of philosophical clarification, and increasing rational grasp of the core of the aesthetic, they will claim as the contingent, transient causal outcome of historical process, fueled by social and economic forces, and having little or nothing to do with the reflection and choices of individual agents. Only very specific conditions — for favored classes, no doubt — will allow a so-called pure and detached aesthetic experience to be attained and enjoyed at leisure. "The aesthetic attitude . . . is a product of the entire history of the field."[9] To claim *more* for such a concept of the aesthetic is — for these critics — falsely to eternalize what is through and through historical. In any case, a substantial amount of recent art itself cannot be comprehended in terms of Kantian and post-Kantian accounts. It is not expected to sustain and reward contemplation, or to be the object of disinterested enjoyment. Nor can stability and continuity be reestablished by reference to art history and extrapolations from it. Such history is itself no more than the bogus rationalizing of the political status quo.

All this cannot fail to put the defender of my Kantian and post-Kantian account into a painful position. If all is causal outcome of historical process, bypassing the thought and witting action of individuals, then I am really being denied the possibility of my counterarguments being taken at their face value as arguments. I also confront the stigma of "reactionary," should I continue to accord serious aesthetic value only to objects that do satisfy my aesthetic-theoretical criteria, and thus to by no means all recent artistic productions. What should I do?

As a first response, I cannot justly be denied the right to make my reasoned defense. My opponents quite obviously do not apply their metaphysic of historical determinism consistently so as to include within its scope their own argumentation and their own alleged insights into historical process. Or if they plead that such historical determination is compatible with the exercise of their rational powers, then that must apply to my powers and my arguments as well. Within the present debate I should want to argue that, short of accepting a metaphysic of historical determinism, I can acknowledge all sorts of historical factors, or possible historical explanations for the rise and fall of aesthetic concepts and theories, without that undermining the *different* enterprise of attempting a rational appraisal of the theories. Historical change may simply bring about conditions in which people can discover, put into effect, and become self-conscious about modes of aesthetic creation and appreciation, the rational justification of which is in no way sabotaged by the occurrence of these empirical conditions at a particular point in time. Nonrelative, objectively valuable insights cannot fail, as occurrences, to be historically datable. But that cannot be news.

A social history of art and of theorizing about art and the aesthetic in general has attractions and value in its own right. It will attract not only Marxists, but also Wittgensteinians who acknowledge that exploring a concept means exploring a whole way of life or a complex "game" that is played, with that concept in a key role. Yet this cannot rule out the distinct and different enquiry, the enquiry whether that is a crazy game to go on playing or one that incorporates insights that make it worth playing today and tomorrow. Of course the out-and-out theorist of historical inevitability wants it both ways: to rule out that normative enquiry *and* to tell the Kant-Schiller theorists that they are playing a crazy game! Here again, as in my first critical argument, my opponents are unable to apply their own theoretical conclusions to their actions in arguing for them.

It can be urged further that it is far from plausible to claim that social and economic forms of explanation are really more illuminating than explanation in distinctively aesthetic terms, when we are considering, for instance, changes of style in the arts, in idiom, or in the vehicle, say, of musical meaning. Changes in the construction of movements in sonata form, for instance, become intelligible only in the detailed internal analysis of the music, not its external nonmusical environment. And if that is so, we are at liberty to set aside anything that irrelevantly deflects our all-too-easily-deflected attention from what goes on in one world to what goes on in another. Moreover, these very general observations must apply not only to the temporal changes within the arts, but equally to theorizing about the arts, and to what would deflect us from that, or occasion a failure of nerve or of confidence in our independent powers of philosophical thought.[10]

Although historical inevitability as a metaphysics is readily shown to be philosophically confused, it is not without harmful practical implications. Through a half-metaphorical, half-literal personification, history becomes an obscure agency, very like fate or destiny, whose ways are no more challengeable than theirs. Through a self-suppression of our freedom we may shirk the difficult, un-modish perspective or decision, telling ourselves that *this* is where history is said to be heading, and hadn't we better move with it?

Thus encouraged, it is possible to go somewhat more on the offensive. I suggest that the chief constituents of our Kantian preferred view are in fact intensifications of indispensable mental activities, activities in which we have an abiding, *necessary* interest. Aesthetic contemplation is basically nothing other than the most vigorous, rapt, undistracted, synoptic awareness. It is maximal awareness in both its scope and intensity. Only a suicidal urge to narrow down, damp down, and ultimately to extinguish conscious life can repudiate that as an ideal. The element of freedom in it is incipiently present in any operation of the mind. In its motility, the active play of attention, freedom is manifesting itself. But one of its fuller realizations lies in the self-sustaining and self-rewarding attentiveness to aesthetic objects and their appraisal through criteria of our own free endorsing. It lies also in realizing and exploiting the endless variety of possible aesthetic perspectives in art and nature. In other words, the constituents are so fundamental that they can be assured by transcendental argument.[11]

That other concept, the disinterestedness of aesthetic experience, is already implicit in what I have just described. It is totally misunderstood if thought of as indifference, lack of interest. And its important moral implications are of course altogether lost in such an account. In fact, it signifies an earnest focusing of attention on the aesthetic object, with the suspending of all self-interested, acquisitive, and manipulatory concerns. Thus understood, it is a close relative of moral openness to the being of another, for that being's own sake.

So I am far from agreeing with Adorno when he writes, "The postulate of disinterestedness debases all art, turning it into a pleasant or useful plaything." Taken in the sense I have sketched out, it is entirely compatible with a powerful emotional response to a work of art—for instance to Kafka's *Metamorphosis*, which Adorno cites.[12] The distinction between art and life, the distinction between the disinterested and the existentially involved, is not thereby annulled.

Consider an aesthetician who accepts both a strictly analytical, metacritical conception of her role, and judges herself obliged to defer, largely, to the verdicts of the art establishment—critics, dealers, museum administrators—as to what today is and is not art. Her task will be seen as limited to practicing analysis on writings about the approved corpus, and on such revised accounts of aesthetic appreciation as that corpus seems to the art world to require. For myself, I am quite unable today to accept that very restricted conception of the legitimate work of aesthetics. If I totally defer to the nonphilosophical art experts, I have certainly to abandon the post-Kantian conceptions, together with their valuable implications for moral and political life in community. So I have the option of possibly rejecting some critical appraisals of contemporary art works—but that involves me also being a critic among critics. Less dogmatically, I may seek a point of reflective equilibrium where, as both philosopher and critic, I can bring my modified views of the aesthetic and my modified reflection about contemporary art objects into harmony.

What in general I cannot avoid is moving freely and constantly from level to level, from the level of metaphysical understanding to the level of metacriticism and to that of art criticism itself. For instance, in the name of a basically metaphysical view of human freedom, I might attack aesthetic and art-critical theorizing that denies the scope of that freedom and thus indirectly impoverishes both appreciation and new creative work, because the options for freedom are not grasped. Or I might criticize art education which, through speaking of social-historical determination far more than of freedom, has the effect at the practical level, not of "wrenching freedom from natural necessity," but contrariwise of imposing its own "irrational domination."

For example, in his contribution to the collection *Analytic Aesthetics*, and chiefly in opposition to arguments of Adorno, Anthony Savile denies that the integrity of the artist, his concern with the truth of the human condition, especially its grimmer aspects, requires him to mirror that grimness in no less grim works of art, as Adorno had claimed. Instead, Savile argues, again looking to Schiller, the artist may freely choose an alternative way. Not at all ignoring the grim reality, he may set over against its turbulence and conflict an image of the most sharply contrasting kind, perhaps an image of beauty, harmony, conflict resolved. Savile's example is from a perceptive critical comment by M. Butor on Mark Rothko's response to the chaotic, value-degrading turmoil of a modern city:

> Into this turbulence an empty space must be inserted . . . so that the spirit can find the tranquillity for its work that it needs.[13]

How right this is. I would add that to read Rothko's work in this way is both an aesthetic-theoretical and an art-critical activity. It is aesthetic-theoretical in its view of the artist's social responsibility and his freedom to detach himself, so as not simply to mirror but to create the image of an alternative ideal. But it is critical also. By no means any and every idyllic image would be properly appraisable as Butor appraised paintings of Rothko. It is as critic before a particular work of art that one has to answer the question: Does this alternative image emerge from deeply felt and pondered experience of the grim reality—has it reckoned with that? Or is it merely evasive and lacking any grip on the reality? For another example, by no means any piece of idyllic pastoral poetry would suffice as a powerful image with which to rebuke a society whose industry pollutes its actual forests and waterways. Here again we touch down on criticism of individual works of art.

It is of course by modernist and late modernist art that the philosopher of life sympathetic to the view I have been defending is more vehemently challenged. He has very frequently to make up his mind what has to yield—a current manifesto or the post-Kantian account—for often they cannot stand together. Where there is talk of the artist's freedom, it may be in terms of total or absolute freedom, rupturing cultural continuity and any sense of a tradition whose riches are relied upon even as they are reworked. Other movements have produced an opposite problem. Instead of narrowing aesthetic attention to the sheer physical object alone, these have "attenuated art's connection with the physical world"[14] — particularly minimalist and conceptual art — and put all the stress upon interpretative idea or theory. With these we are a very long way from understanding an art work as a complex unity which sustains and rewards contemplative attention.

Obviously we cannot here enter critical debate over any of these movements, or make pronouncements in the absence of individual art works. But we can note that each extreme gives legitimate work for the philosopher-critic. On the one side, if the vital thing is the idea content, then the coherence or incoherence, the importance or fatuity of the ideas, is a very proper concern of the philosopher, whatever the verdicts of the art establishment. If, on the other side, attention is focused only upon the pure physicality of a work, then the question needs to be raised, by art historians, aestheticians, and critics, whether *pure* here entails thin, impoverished, undernourished, attenuated. Discontinuity is a tempting goal for radical aesthetic initiative, a gesture of absolute freedom from the domination of the past, but it can be purchased at a very high cost.

It is worth noting that although a word like *pure* can seem to work on the side of freedom — shaking free from encumbering tradition, freeing painting from slavish mimesis — it can work quite the other way. It can be used to imply that if a style of art is locatable on a spectrum or continuum, one extreme point of which is a clearly inappropriate ideal (such as *trompe l'oeil*, photographical realism, in visual art), then in the interests of purity and of logic, artists *ought* to work at the other extreme point, where the purification is complete. The logic in such a statement is often very dubious: to urge a movement to its "logical conclusions" can be highly illogical where that means taking to a one-sided extreme. For all we can tell by theorizing, artists may work most effectively at various points *between* the poles of imitation and of abstract design. And there have been critics who urged the exclusion of concern with any features of painting which are also features of other media and not unique to painting—leading, for instance, to a cult of flatness. This is a form of argument no more convincing in the field of art than in ethics. Compare: "What is important about man must be what is unique to him, qua man." His reason and creativity? Fine; but what about his unique capacity for cruelty and malice? Not all that confers distinctiveness also confers distinction.

I instance these briefly here, because they are all sad ways in which our thinking about art can reduce, rather than augment, aesthetic freedom. Elsewhere I have written about the very similar curtailment of freedom to respond variously to nature as aesthetic object, where sociological generalization about, say, the infrequency today of much popular reference to nature as "sublime" or "awesome" is hardened into a social-historical deterministic claim that "to us the sublime is no longer available." We should refuse to be bullied. To some of us it does remain a live possibility for experience.

All of the above could be taken as a sermon on Schiller's text: "Spirit cannot be injured except by what robs it of its freedom."

II

In my initial outline of values of common concern to the aesthetic enterprise and to the moral community, I spoke of the aesthetic attitude as contemplative in contrast to rapacious, disinterested in contrast to self-interested, and as one "in which respect for other being plays a vital part." I want, then, to turn next to that respect for the being of others, above all for personal being, and its role in art and morality. This value too comes under threat and, long familiar though it is, needs defending.

We are obviously here still in the realm of Kantian ideas, particularly in the case of respect for persons as the bearers of freedom and reason. That needs no quotation. For Schiller, the aesthetic makes society possible: ". . . only the aesthetic mode of communication unites society, because it relates to that which is common to all." Where our aesthetic nature is allowed predominance, people "make their way, with undismayed simplicity and tranquil innocence . . . free . . . of the compulsion to infringe the freedom of others in order to assert their own." Aestheticizing, as involving recognition of and respect for the freedom and worth of the other, brings to Schiller a variety of fundamental transformations of human life. For instance, desire is transmuted into love: "out of a selfish exchange of lust there grows a generous interchange of affection." Thus, analogously and generally, beauty works to resolve the tensions of society as such, seeking to "reconcile the gentle with the violent in the moral world."[15]

The theme of respect for other being, in its basically Kantian form, has to be extended. Such extension is a necessary development of the movements of thought we have just sampled in Schiller. Environmental ethics, as well as aesthetics, has recently been counseling a respect for the natural world, its forms of life, its wilderness, its forests and coasts. The movement from human domination *by* nature all too readily passes to its opposite extreme, human domination *of* nature, so far as that lies within technologically heightened human powers. Between these extremes is the condition of *having*, but not *using*, the power to manipulate and destroy; instead, respecting and cherishing other being.[16]

A further extension is suggested in an analogy affirmed by several writers in aesthetics, the analogy between our attitudes to persons and our attitudes to works of art. In both, we look for meaning in their movements, gestures, and presentations. We show respect for a work of art when we refuse to see it as a disposable message to be read and discarded; when we see it instead as an inherently valuable, irreplaceable artifact, whose message, if any, is individualized by its embodiment in that unique object. If it is obscure and difficult, then it is difficult as persons can be difficult. We are tantalized, baffled maybe, but we respect their enigmatic otherness. In relation to art of the past, such respect for individual work and for tradition checks the artist's freedom to repudiate the past, in order to make an untrammeled personal statement. So checked, this statement may well be saved from being aesthetically thin and meager.

My harping on writings of the 1790s may suggest that no modern support for some of these ideas can be found. Turn then to Adorno's *Aesthetic Theory*, whose author would have disclaimed a fair amount of what I am arguing for. Yet he writes:

There is a grain of validity even in a contemplative attitude towards art, inasmuch as it underscores the important posture of art's turning away from immediate praxis. . . .

Art is like a plenipotentiary of a type of praxis that is better than the prevailing praxis of society, dominated as it is by brutal self-interest.

And again, much later in the book, when discussing the relation between arts and sciences:

Crudeness of thinking is the inability to make differentiations in the analysis of something that is being studied. [It is] an aesthetic category as well as a cognitive one. . . .

This has moral implications, in that brutality against things is potentially brutality against human beings. Art by definition negates crudeness, the subjective nucleus of evil, coming out on the side of its opposite, i.e., the ideal of elaboration.

It is through this — and not through the pronouncement of moral tenets . . .— that art partakes of morality, linking it to the ideal of a more humane society.[17]

Differentiating, discriminating, affirming, or celebrating, rather than brutally manipulating or destroying other being — all are facets of the aesthetic-moral value of respect as I am interpreting it. To take further another element in what I read from Schiller, the aesthetic can work toward assimilating or sublimating the subpersonal into personal life, the life of persons in relation. Art spiritualizes the world, in the sense of appropriating and making communicable the objects and thought objects of the human life world. It *is* the personal refusing to surrender to its enemies, subpersonal forces and death — so long as it can. Tragedy at its best epitomizes this most fully and momentously.

Whence then comes the threat to respect, as a value of art and of community? It comes wherever those movements are thrown into reverse, where very fine discrimination and differentiation are replaced by simplifications that distort and misrepresent, and by blurring of significant differences, most often in the interest of political or religious ideology. That can happen both in art and in criticism of art.

An even more obvious and serious threat arises also if art and thought about art reverse the spiritualizing movement, the movement from subpersonal to personal, fragmenting the unity of the person. A critic has no right to complain if an artist chooses to show the disintegration of an individual or society or state; but complain he may if an artist's or writer's *oeuvre* consistently beams upon her audience an image of humanity that degrades and reduces the personal as such. All our putative other-concerns are allegedly self-concerns, and that self no more than the loosest assemblage of demanding instincts. All our loves are lusts, and those lusts brutal.

I am thinking of some works of Genet, of some postwar German Expressionists, and of artists whose sense of identity seems not to lie even in a generalized sexuality, but looks back — regressing still further — to what a Freudian would call the "anal" stage. There was, some years ago, a Parisian exhibit with the ambiguous title, "Mer(d)e de l'artiste."

The link in this area between the values of art and of morality are close enough for a moral critique to be entirely in order. For putting this kind of reduction in moral terms: there is an implied reversal of the order of development of culture and reason. From the level of morality, including respect for persons as such, we collapse down first to the level of reflective self-concern, and from there to the fragmented self, now only a bundle of querulous instincts. The upper levels are regarded as pretentious, elitist, sham. Moral community is no serious option; as an ideal it is obliterated. The community, improperly so called, presupposed as audience, is one in which the personal dimension all but vanishes. Art's fall is particularly terrible if we see art as potentially the agent of enhancing personal life, and as working, in such cases, as an agent of reduction instead.[18]

To comment on this at all is again obviously to break away from the purely second-order conception of aesthetics. The question demands also to be raised, whether such an artist or writer as I have just described is in a state of self-contradiction? He is surely denying, implicitly, in his picture of humankind, capabilities which he cannot fail to be manifesting, himself, in his own activity of painting or writing.

III

One of the principal ways in which we manifest respect for personhood and for the freedom of persons is by centering our dealings with other persons upon appeal to reason and reasonableness rather than upon nonrational manipulation. Indeed, the concept of appeal to reason and the respect due to persons are surely internally related. Yet another important value for moral community, the value of reasonableness, is also a value that plays an important role in aesthetic activity, one that we have strong justification for retaining there, though it is often occluded. It too needs careful defense against threats from without and hazards from within.

In the Third Critique, Kant argues that, despite the ultimate reference of judgments of taste to the experience of individual subjects, to claim for an object aesthetic value or beauty is to make "a rightful claim upon the assent of all. . . ." Art-critical discourse is a reasonable appeal to persons to bring their aesthetic judgments into mutual accord, without loss of autonomy. It is an appeal, finally, to their individual judgment; and there is to be no nonrational deference. Kant acknowledges that this is not a field in which we can expect proofs in support of our judgments. Yet, in criticism, reason has vital work to do, not least in the assembling and comparing of concrete examples: the goal is "the rectification and extension of our judgments of taste."[19] The pursuit of aesthetic criticism benefits not only our discrimination among works of art and our openness to their qualities; it also benefits the life of reason and reasonableness in the human community as such. To quote Selim Kemal once more: for Kant to represent aesthetic activity as "dialogue with other subjects," emphasis has shifted

> from a concern with consciousness to one with community.
> . . . The community is a unity whose public standards are drawn from and respect the human capacity for reason and feeling. [It replaces arbitrary and conflictful egoistic relationships] with a unified, intersubjective and persuasive dialogue between autonomous individuals.[20]

The immense range of applications of reason and reasonableness vis-à-vis the arts needs to be unpacked a little more. Some of these applications are commonly misidentified as the work of sheer feeling or intuition. Appraisal concepts drawn, for instance, from high-level aesthetic generalization or from genre categories yield only the most schematic of starting points. Reasonable critical discourse about a particular art work may require interpretative analysis and detailed comparisons and analogies with other instances of its general kind. The individuality of works of art prevents any instance serving as an archetypal ideal, since divergences from features of any putative ideal may be aesthetically justifiable in the particular case. And we do, rationally, justify them by indicating the positive role these features play in the total art work before us. *Indicating* may mean describing the features, and describing counterfactual, imaginary art works which, lacking just those features, would illuminatingly fail to achieve the same, valued effect. Or we may outline a fanciful program for a passage of music that suggests a way of hearing it so as to bring out an expressive quality that was being lost in performance.[21]

What then should be said about threats and dangers with respect to this value of reasonableness?

First of all it may be objected that we are ignoring feeling and emotion. But feeling in art is expressed through highly specific perception of objective features and is thus the possible subject of rational enquiry. It is not at all a free-floating aura detached from chord sequences or text, or from juxtaposed images, forms, colors. Emotions, by now familiarly, involve situation appraisals, cognitive interpretations, as part of their essence, and as such can be reasoned over. We think as well as feel our way into aesthetic particulars, as we move from work to work, from character to character in a fiction, from one character's perspective on the world to another's—always fallibly, with need for self-criticism and self-correction. And such exercises of reason—attentive, flexible, empathizing—are of course equally necessary to the moral context of our understanding of self and others. Necessary, yes; but I cannot say "sufficient," since we all know that it is possible to read Rilke in the evening and tend the gas chambers in the morning. The insulation of these spheres from each other is one form of human perversity.

Furthermore, it is a danger of our time that we do not carry reasonableness far enough. Ready acceptance can be counted upon for claims about the work of reason in delineating and clarifying alternative perspectives on the world and imaginatively occupying them. It is in the borderland between aesthetic and nonaesthetic, between imaginative visiting and existential appropriating of perspectives, ways of looking into the world, that reason may relinquish its hold too early. From the legitimacy of art's presenting any perspective whatever, we may wrongly infer that all are equally justifiable, equally legitimate, in life; or that none are. Such an inference offers easy support to moral relativism. But to set the matter out in such simple stark terms makes clear how unwarranted is any move in that direction. For we have no grounds for supposing that the limits of reason and the limits of reasonableness are reached in the sensitive communicating and sharing of perspectives. That same complex of rational activities — analogy, metaphor, case-by-case comparison — can combine in the fields of practical and moral deliberation. Our imagination may work too much under the image of the duck/rabbit, the picture preference. But not every rabbit picture is equally reasonably seen also as a duck.

A third domain in which reasonableness may not be carried far enough is, very obviously, the domain of talk about art itself, particularly in manifestoes for new movements, and in art criticism more generally. Dialogue is frustrated in these contexts if a writer seeks to bully the public into acquiescence, or use nonrational, mystifying, perhaps pseudophilosophical persuasions on behalf of his artists. Once more, the philosopher of art should not shirk from the task of liberating the critical dialogue again, by patiently seeking clarification — but also, where necessary, calling nonsense its name and refusing to subordinate individual aesthetic judgment to art world authority.

A fourth hazard arises in implementing the value of reasonableness, if we fail to operate with it in conjunction with other relevant values. Were we, for instance, to link the aesthetic worth of a work of art with the extent of attainable agreement over its pleasurability, then the accolades would go to currently popular music, to the sensational bestseller, and to its film version. Supposing that it is in shareability that we are basically interested, and the social cohesiveness that is furthered by dialogue over shareable pleasures in art, it would follow, as Anthony Savile put it in

Aesthetic Reconstructions, that "the interest that our need for social cohesiveness gives rise to is no more than . . . an interest in
finding *something or other* we might all take pleasure in."[22] And
the notion of there being critical power of discrimination (or difficult art) is quickly lost in an anti-elitist slide. That is to say, reasonableness should not be taken as pursuit of the most readily
shareable. We are noting the sad effects that would ensue from
accepting a rather tempting shortcut to enhance the community
value associated with reasonableness: it would impair the values
of art, and through loss of concern with quality, impair the life
of community itself, if less directly and in the longer term.[23]

    Finally, it must be the concrete particular work that is the
central concern of these specifically aesthetic exercises in reasonableness. The relevant reasons are reasons for taking a work one
way rather than another, for grasping the point of the work, for
understanding why it has the appearance, the sound, the shape
it does. If no intelligible story whatever can be offered, we are entitled to suspect that a work is empty. If much is said about it,
yet little or none of that can be read back into the look or the sound
of the work itself, but remains external to it, we are entitled to
suspect that theorizing has supplanted art.

IV

    Freedom, autonomy, respect, reasonableness — to this point
I have been considering certain values and forms of experience of
fundamental importance to the community's moral and aesthetic
life. Similar consideration needs to be given also to certain basic
religious modes of experience, which the arts can manifest with
power and vividness. I wish to allude very briefly to a sample of
these. I am concerned with art's power to adumbrate generalized but vital aspects of religious experience or aspiration, partly
through certain expressive potentialities of the art media, and partly
through formal features of the arts, but with little dependence on
representational content or message. Among such aspects, the first
will be conceptions of transcendence which art can keep before
the imagination, even when formal religion falters, and even in
the absence of any firm metaphysical assurance about the existence

and nature of any deity, as conceived by traditional supernatural theism.

The paintings of Caspar David Friedrich, for instance, convey a haunting sense of mystery, of an infinite leading beyond the boundaries of experience, and yet still of strange, indefinable concern to us. They do so far less by overt Christian symbolism than by the use of images from the natural world, for instance by the sea's horizon and the sky toward which the monk gazes, in *Monk by the Sea*, or towards which his sailing ships recede. In his considerably different way, Samuel Palmer could paint an everyday pastoral landscape, modest hills, sky, moon, the hint of a village, and make these seem a "frontispiece of eternity." Nor do such intimations of transcendence belong to a tradition now only in the past. It continues into our own century with painters like Paul Klee and Lyonel Feininger, who reworked expressively just those motifs I mentioned in Friedrich. At that same time, to quote Robert Rosenblum, Graham Sutherland "was studying and paraphrasing the art of Samuel Palmer." To this still lively tradition belong also Max Ernst, Piet Mondrian, and once again, Rothko.[24] In different idioms, all present images either of a circumambient mystery or of a dissolution of particular forms in a void that yet is not sheer negativity, but may be apprehended as unbounded, primordial, creative energy.

There is high painterly skill here as well as a capacity for elemental experience. Minute differences distinguish a visionary landscape from a trite pastoral pastiche, a religious void from a secular blank.

Such successes in the evocation of transcendence by the arts can survive a philosophical critique of the theory, the conceptualized theology, in which the artists may interpret their own beliefs.

Here once more, however, certain very familiar threats and challenges are encountered today. Apologists of the avant garde have wanted to repudiate the Romantic tradition I have been sampling, seeing it as a betrayal of a secularization process that we should be completing, not reversing. Artists as creators should rather confirm their new overt role as ousting the supposed divine creator, and reign in God's stead.[25]

These sentiments may well be applauded by a skeptical philosopher. He will remind us of the numerous critical arguments

mounted over the last half-century against the validity of a concept of divine transcendence. What starts as a most impressive and
awesome idea reveals itself, with more specific elaboration, as sub-
limely empty. In the interest of divine perfection, and of due dis-
tancing from the realm of objects and spatiotemporality, in retreat
from any finitizing, the concept loses all determinateness, all
positive content. After analysis we are left with a void indeed! Yet,
of course, what I have reminded you of, as a typical skeptic's argument, can very largely be re-presented and defended in religious
terms, even if undogmatically. It does indeed derogate from transcendence to envisage it anthropomorphically, or as objectively
existent in any sense appropriate to objects in the life world. We
degrade it no less, if we think of it as operating in another realm.
We can think and speak of the transcendent chiefly as a direction of transformation — of our values, our vision of this world —
in terms, that is, of transcending. Beyond that, we are agnostic,
silent.[26]

In that minimal positive account of transcendence, the role
of the arts to sustain and intensify the wonderment appropriate
to it cannot be exaggerated. Its meagerness of content is little em-
barrassment, since it discards the real religious embarrassments,
superstition, an ethic of authority, and the intolerance that readily goes with it. In a word, I am saying that nonconceptual evocations of transcendence in art can bring nearer to fulfillment
certain basic religious movements of the mind (for instance, from
world to God) than is possible within the conceptual systems of
theology.

In response to the secularizing apologist of the avant garde
I should want to say that there is no single and authoritative movement towards secularization. We have something immensely more
complex than that — strands of analysis of concepts of transcendence — some of which can be interpreted in a skeptical, secularizing way or in a nondogmatically religious way. Each mode of interpretation takes on depth and convincingness, when set into the
great complex of other evidences and arguments for and against
religious or secular positions. I see that overall dispute as bringing
me into agreement more often with the secular view than with
the world religions. Yet the outcome is not apparent, and gives
us no entitlement to speak of completing a secularizing process.

That again is a crude simplification of complex matters for free decision by individuals, not a trend to take — as a good progressive always should! — to its logical conclusion, *à l'outrance*, for better or (more likely) for worse.

Earlier I argued against reductionism of the personal to the subpersonal, in art as in moral relationships. Here I want to hold my ground in not accepting a reductionism of the transcendent, and transcending movements of thought, by which such elusive and unconceptualizable evocations are reduced to their spatio-temporal elements or props and the wonder is dissipated.

There exist other striking areas of phenomenological overlap between the fields of art and religion. Some years ago I wrote about one in an article called "Time-Transcendence." I argued for an illuminating analogy between God's eternity understood as synoptic grasp of the entire temporal process — *totem simul*, as distinct from sempiternity; and our own very limited but real synoptic grasping of temporal works of art. A poem held in the mind as a unity, and a musical movement whose individual notes are not heard and lost but held and gathered in the mind as a meaningful whole, are illustrations.[27]

I shall end by indicating yet a third instance where our thinking about God is paralleled in the microcosm of an art work. On the side of art, two key concepts are involved in interrelation: first, a concern with life, enlivening, energy, the dynamic; second, a concern with the contemplative, disengagement, profound peace of mind, the still center. On the side of theism, theology has frequently attributed to God incessant creative activity and vitality, and at the same time motionlessness, rest, and peace. God is at the convergence of these values, at their infinite intensity.

To speak of stillness in art is not at all to cancel the awareness of vitality. For instance, Schopenhauer claimed that although aesthetic experience is "detached from . . . the will, [it is] nevertheless active with the highest degree of energy"; and for Schiller, the mood in which a genuine work of art should release us was one of "equanimity and freedom of the spirit, combined with power and vigor."[28]

The fusion of these values in the nature of God was never more sharply expressed than by Dionysius the Areopagite in his treatise, *The Divine Names*. God, as supreme goodness and beauty, is above all rest and motion, yet is also "that through which all rest and motion come." Again, divine movement combines "emanation and productive stillness." "In his eternal motion God remains at rest."[29]

The interdependence of the two forms of value is intelligible enough: maximum scope and intensity of awareness, but without loss of integration. The pursuit of stimulus, heightening of awareness, requires a center of stillness, an origin for its ordering perspective, not itself in the field of stimuli. Conversely, supposing calm and tranquillity are necessarily desirable; if they are one-sidedly developed, they would carry a threat of peace at the expense of heightened consciousness. Hence the need for the two in tension.

Once more, then, I am arguing that we have in this duality a high aesthetic value that offers insight into, and has power to sustain, that remarkable religious conception, the idea of a divine perfection in terms of life, energy, and stillness. Am I suggesting that even if the specifically religious imagination today finds such a conception elusive or irrelevant, we can treasure at least its aesthetic analogues, and that they can continue to witness to it even in a predominantly secular time?

Partly that; but its manifestation in art too is not without its detractors. By no means every style and movement in art today will accept the contemplative ideal, though some will. To attempt another defense against current threats, therefore, needs another essay. In any case, a concern for the art of one's own day hardly entails an ignoring of the art of the past, which does present countless instantiations of that dual ideal. It will suffice to remind you (by way of coda) of two such. The first works at several levels: it is a literary-philosophical comment upon a work of sculpture; and the sculpture was taken as religious art, the representation of a goddess. And the whole belongs to the work of aesthetics from which I have often been quoting—Schiller's *Letters on the Aesthetic Education of Man.*

> It is not Grace, nor is it yet Dignity, which speaks to us from the superb countenance of a Juno Ludovisi; it is both at once. While the woman-god demands our veneration, the god-like woman kindles our love. . . . The whole figure reposes and

dwells in itself, a creation completely self-contained. . . . Ir-resistibly moved and drawn [that is, by the qualities that kindle love], kept at a distance [by the divine, daunting self-sufficiency], we find ourselves [at once] in a state of utter repose and supreme agitation, and there results that wondrous stir-ring of the heart for which the mind has no conception nor speech any name.[30]

I draw a second example from *The Prelude* by Wordsworth. Wordsworth put that tension between stillness and motion at the heart of his account of the sublime. He claimed expressly that there can be no sublimity without a sense of repose. It is present in Book VI, where he writes of the "immeasurable heights / Of woods de-caying, never to be decay'd, / The stationary blasts of waterfalls." Describing the Alpine pass in Book VI, he wrote:

> Black drizzling crags that spake by the way-side
> As if a voice were in them, the sick sight
> And giddy prospect of the raving stream,
> The unfetter'd clouds, and region of the heavens,
> *Tumult and peace*, the darkness and the light
> Were all like workings of one mind, the features
> Of the same face, blossoms upon one tree,
> Characters of the Great Apocalypse,
> The types and symbols of Eternity,
> Of first and last, and midst, and without end.[31]

NOTES

1. Immanuel Kant, *Critique of Judgment*, trans. Meredith (New York: Oxford University Press, 1961; originally published in 1790), sec. 53, p. 191; sec. 49, p. 176; sec. 59, pp. 223f.

2. Friedrich Schiller, *On the Aesthetic Education of Man, In a Series of Letters*, ed. and trans. E. M. Wilkinson and L. A. Willoughby (New York: Oxford University Press, 1967; originally published in 1794–95), Letter 26, p. 191; Letter 25, p. 185.

3. Nicholas Wolterstorff, in *Analytic Aesthetics*, ed. R. Shuster-man (Oxford and New York: Basil Blackwell, 1989), ch. 3, p. 44.

4. See also R. Wollheim, *Painting as an Art* (London: Thames & Hudson, 1987), pp. 14–16.

5. Selim Kemal, *Kant and Fine Art* (Oxford: Clarendon Press, 1986), pp. 275–76.

6. Ian Ground, *Art or Bunk?* (Bristol: Bristol Classical Press, 1989), p. 121.

7. Sandy Nairne, *State of the Art: Ideas and Images in the 1980s* (London: Chatto & Windus, 1987), p. 126.

8. Ibid., pp. 29, 50, 42.

9. Pierre Bourdieu, in *Analytic Aesthetics*, ed. Shusterman, p. 156.

10. Relevant here is R. Scruton, *The Aesthetic Understanding* (London: Methuen, 1983), esp. pp. 170–74.

11. There are echoes here of John Findlay's account of the aesthetic.

12. T. W. Adorno, *Aesthetic Theory* (London: Routledge & Kegan Paul, 1984).

13. M. Butor, quoted in Anthony Savile, in *Analytic Aesthetics*, ed. Shusterman, p. 141.

14. P. Meeson, in *Dialectics and Humanism* 15, no. 1–2 (1988 – published in Warsaw): 189f.

15. Schiller, *Aesthetic Education*, Letter 27, pp. 213, 215, 219.

16. Benedict Spinoza is a better guide here than Kant or Schiller. See Stuart Hampshire, *Two Theories of Morality* (New York: Oxford University Press, 1977), pp. 90–95: "an exultation and respect before the order and variety of nature" (p. 91 [Hampshire's words]).

17. Adorno, *Aesthetic Theory*, p. 329.

18. See also A. O'Hear's book, *The Element of Fire* (London: Routledge & Kegan Paul, 1988), with which I am very much in sympathy.

19. Kant, *Critique of Judgment*, sec. 7, p. 52; sec. 32, p. 137; sec. 33, p. 140; sec. 34, p. 141.

20. Kemal, *Kant and Fine Art*, pp. 151f.

21. For another account in the same spirit, see David Best, *Feeling and Reason in the Arts* (London: Allen & Unwin, 1985), ch. 2, pp. 12ff.

22. Anthony Savile, *Aesthetic Reconstructions* (Oxford and New York: Basil Blackwell, 1987), p. 166.

23. The best account known to me of "practical reasonableness" is in John Finnis, *Natural Law and Natural Rights* (Oxford: Clarendon Press, 1980), ch. 5, pp. 100ff.

24. I am much indebted to Robert Rosenblum's study, *Modern Painting and the Northern Romantic Tradition* (London: Thames & Hudson, 1975). The quoted words are from p. 162.

25. See, for instance, Peter Fuller, *Theoria: Art and the Absence of Grace* (London: Chatto & Windus, 1988), pp. 207, 210.

26. These are themes in Jaspers's philosophical-religious thinking. See, for example, Karl Jaspers, *Philosophy* (1969; originally published in 1932), vol. 1.

27. R. W. Hepburn, "Time-Transcendence," in R. W. Hepburn, *Wonder* (Edinburgh: Edinburgh University Press, 1984), ch. 6, pp. 108–30.

28. Arthur Schopenhauer, *The World as Will and Representation*, trans. E. F. J. Payne (New York: Dover, 1958), vol. 2, p. 374; and Schiller, *Aesthetic Education*, Letter 22, pars. 3–4.

29. Dionysius, *The Divine Names*, trans. G. E. Rolt, pp. 100ff., 106, 168.

30. Schiller, *Aesthetic Education*, Letter 15, pp. 108–9.

31. William Wordsworth, *The Prelude*, book 6, lines 556–58, 563–72 (emphasis added).

3

Wittgenstein on Religious Belief

HILARY PUTNAM

MY TOPIC IS WITTGENSTEIN'S THREE "Lectures on Religious Belief."[1]
We do not have the full text of these lectures. What we have are
notes taken by students, and these notes undoubtedly take up many
fewer pages than printed versions of the lectures themselves would
have. But these notes are a valuable source nonetheless. For one
thing, in these lectures the students often make objections or suggestions as to what Wittgenstein should say, and very often Wittgenstein's refusal to accept what the students thought he should
say tells us a great deal about Wittgenstein's philosophy, and about
the ways in which even the best of his students were tempted to
misinterpret it.

I was first led to study the published notes on the "Lectures
on Religious Belief" by their subject, but besides the interest they
have for anyone who has thought about the subject of religious
language and religious belief, they also have a great interest for
anyone who is interested in understanding the work of the later
Wittgenstein. They were given, in fact, in the summer of 1938,
when the views of "the latter Wittgenstein" were in process of development. But these lectures by no means bear their meaning on
their sleeve. Even if we had the full text of what Wittgenstein said
in that room in Cambridge in 1938, I suspect we would be deeply
puzzled by these lectures, and as it is, we only have twenty printed
pages of student notes summarizing three lectures.

The very first of the three lectures already sets the interpretative problem before us. What Wittgenstein says in this first
lecture is very much contrary to received opinion in linguistic
philosophy, and there is an obvious problem as to how it is to be

understood. In this lecture, Wittgenstein considers a number of religious utterances — not utterances about God, but about the afterlife, or the Last Judgment. One example is, "An Austrian general said to someone, 'I shall think of you after my death, if that should be possible.'" Wittgenstein says, "We can imagine one group who would find this ludicrous, another who wouldn't."[2]

Again, Wittgenstein imagines someone asking him if he believes in a Last Judgment, and on the first page of the published notes, Wittgenstein says, "Suppose that I say that the body will rot, and another says, 'No, particles will rejoin in a thousand years and there will be a resurrection of you.'" Wittgenstein's comment is, "If someone said, 'Wittgenstein, do you believe in this?' I'd say, 'No.' 'Do you contradict the man?' I'd say, 'No.' . . . 'Would you say, I believe the opposite, or there is no reason to suppose such a thing?' I'd say, 'Neither.'"[3] In short — and perhaps this is the only thing that is absolutely clear about these lectures — Wittgenstein believes that the religious person and the atheist talk past one another.

I remember that the first time I had lunch with one of the greatest students of comparative religion, Wilfred Cantwell Smith, Smith said to me that when the religious person says, "I believe there is a God," and the atheist says, "I don't believe there is a God," they do not affirm and deny the same thing. Wittgenstein makes the same point. Religious discourse is commonly viewed by atheists as prescientific or "primitive" discourse which has somehow strangely — due to human folly and superstition — managed to survive into the age of the digital computer and the neutron bomb. Wittgenstein and Smith clearly believe no such thing. Wittgenstein's picture is not that the believer makes a claim and the atheist asserts its negation. It is as if religious discourse were somehow incommensurable, to employ a much-abused word. But there are many theories of incommensurability, and the problem is to decide in what way Wittgenstein means to deny the commensurability of religious and nonreligious discourse.

The first lecture provides us with a number of clues. When a question is an ordinary empirical question, the appropriate attitude is often not to say "I believe" or "I don't believe," but to say "Probably not" or "Probably yes" or "I'm not sure." Wittgenstein uses the example of someone's saying, "There is a German airplane overhead." If Wittgenstein were to reply, "Possibly; I'm not sure," one would say that the two speakers were "fairly near." But what if someone says, "I believe in the Last Judgment," and Wittgenstein replies, "Well, I'm not so sure. Possibly"? Wittgenstein says, "You would say that there is an enormous gulf between us."[4] For a typical nonbeliever, the Last Judgment isn't even a possibility.

I don't think that Wittgenstein is denying that there is a state of mind in which someone on the verge of a conversion might suddenly stop and say, "What if there is a Last Judgment?" But I think that Wittgenstein would deny that this is at all like "Possibly there is a German airplane overhead."

Wittgenstein distinguishes religious beliefs partly by what he calls their unshakability. Speaking again of the person who believes in a Last Judgment, Wittgenstein says,

> . . . he has what you might call an unshakable belief. It will show not by reasoning, or by appeals to ordinary grounds for belief, but rather by regulating for all of his life.
>
> This is a very much stronger fact. Foregoing pleasures, always appealing to this picture, this in one sense must be called the firmest of all beliefs, because the man risks things on account of it which he would not do on things which are by far better established for him, although he distinguishes between things established and not well established.[5]

In understanding these remarks I think it is important to know that although Wittgenstein presents himself in these lectures as a nonbeliever, we know from the other posthumous writings published as *Culture and Value* that Wittgenstein had a deep respect for religious belief, that he thought a great deal about religious belief, especially about Christianity, and that in particular he paid a great deal of attention to the writings of Kierkegaard, especially the *Concluding Unscientific Postscript*. The man who has an unshakable belief in the Last Judgment and lets it regulate for all his life, although he is quite willing to admit that the Last Judgment is not an established fact, sounds like a Christian after Kierkegaard's own heart.[6] Yet Kierkegaard himself wrote that "faith has in every moment the infinite dialectic of uncertainty present with it."[7] It would be ludicrous to suppose that inner struggles with the issue of religious belief are something that Wittgenstein did not know. When he takes the unshakability of a religious belief as one of its characteristics, he does not mean that a genuine religious belief is always and at every moment free from doubt. Kierkegaard spoke of faith as a state to be repeatedly reentered, and not as a state in which one can permanently stay. But I think that Kierkegaard would agree with Wittgenstein — and that Wittgenstein is here agreeing with Kierkegaard — that religious belief "regulates for all" in the believer's life, even though that person's religious belief may alternate with doubt. In this respect it is different from an empirical belief. If I confidently believe that a certain way is the right way to build a bridge, then I will set out building the bridge; but if I come to have doubts, I will not go on building the bridge in that way (unless I am a crooked contractor). I will halt the construction and run further tests and make calculations.

Wittgenstein uses an interesting example:

> Suppose you had two people, and one of them, when he had to decide which course to take, thought of retribution and the other did not. One person might for instance be inclined to take everything that happened to him as a reward or punishment, and another person doesn't think of it at all.
>
> If he is ill, he may think, "What have I done to deserve this?" This is one way of thinking of retribution. Another way is, he thinks in a general way whenever he is ashamed of himself: "This will be punished."
>
> Take two people, one of whom talks of his behavior and what happens to him in terms of retribution; the other one does not. These people think entirely differently. Yet so far you can't say they believe different things.
>
> It is this way. If someone said, "Wittgenstein, you don't take illness as a punishment, so what do you believe?" I'd say, "I don't have any thoughts of punishment."
>
> There are these entirely different ways of thinking — which needn't be expressed by one person saying one thing, another person saying another thing.[8]

I think we take this example in the wrong way if we suppose that the person who thinks of life in terms of retribution is supposed to be what we ordinarily call a religious believer. The example doesn't depend on whether he or she is or is not. What Wittgenstein means to bring out by the example is that one's life may be organized by very different pictures. And he means to suggest that religion has more to do with the kind of picture that one allows to organize one's life than it does with expressions of belief. As Wittgenstein says, summing up this example, "What we call believing in a Judgment Day or not believing in a Judgment Day — the expression of belief may play an absolutely minor role."[9]

Wittgenstein also contrasts the basis upon which one forms empirical beliefs and the basis upon which one forms religious beliefs, and he says, "Reasons look entirely different from normal reasons" in the religious case. "They are, in a way, quite inconclusive." He contrasts two cases: the case of someone who believes that something that fits the description of the Last Judgment will in fact happen, years and years in the future, and who believes this on the basis of what we would call scientific evidence, and a religious belief which "might in fact fly in the face of such a forecast and say, 'No, there it will break down.'" Wittgenstein says that if a scientist told him that there would be a Last Judgment in a thousand years, and that he had to forego all pleasures because of such a forecast, that he, Wittgenstein, "wouldn't budge." But the person whose belief in such a forecast was religious and not scientific "would fight for his life not to be dragged into the fire." "No induction. Terror. That is, as it were, part of the substance of the belief."[10]

I have presented a number of quotations to give you some sense of the texture of these notes.[11] But what seems most important in this first lecture is the repeated claim that the relation between Wittgenstein (who thoroughly conceals his own struggle with or against religious belief in these lectures) and the believer is not one of contradiction. Wittgenstein says again:

> If you ask me whether or not I believe in a Judgment Day in the sense in which religious people have belief in it, I wouldn't say, "No, I don't believe there will be such a thing." It would seem to me utterly crazy to say this.
> And then I give an explanation. I don't believe in —. But then the religious person never believes in what I describe.
> I can't say. I can't contradict that person.
> In one sense I understand all he says. The English words

"God," "separate," etc., I understand. I could say, "I don't believe in this." And that would be true. Meaning I haven't got these thoughts, or anything that hangs together with them. But not that I could contradict the thing.[12]

At this point, a number of possible interpretations of what Wittgenstein is saying might occur to one.

1. I already mentioned the Kuhnian idea of incommensurability. Perhaps Wittgenstein thinks that religious language and ordinary empirical language are incommensurable forms of discourse. The nonreligious person simply can't understand the religious person.
2. The religious person and the nonreligious person can understand one another, but the nonreligious person is using language literally and the religious person is using it in some nonliteral way, perhaps emotively, or to "express an attitude."
3. Ordinary discourse is "cognitive" and the religious person is making some kind of "noncognitive" use of language.

What I shall try to show in the light of these lectures, and especially the third and concluding lecture, is that Wittgenstein regards the first as a useless thing to say, and the second and third as simply wrong. This will, of course, not solve the interpretative problem, but it will in a sense sharpen it and make it interesting. If Wittgenstein is not saying one of the standard things about religious language — for example, that it expresses false prescientific theories, or that it is noncognitive, or that it is emotive, or that it is incommensurable — then what is he saying, and how is it possible for him to avoid all of these standard alternatives? Still more important, how does he think we, both religious people and nonreligious people, are to think about religious language? What sort of a model is Wittgenstein offering us for reflection on what is always a very important and very difficult, and sometimes a very divisive, part of human life?

Superstition, Religious Belief, Incommensurability

In the second lecture Wittgenstein discusses the difference between the use of pictures to represent people — including biblical subjects, such as Noah and the ark — and the use of pictures to represent God. "You might ask this question, did Michelangelo think that Noah and the ark looked like this and that God creating Adam looked like this? He wouldn't have said that God or Adam looked as they look in this picture."[13]

Interestingly, Wittgenstein says:

> In general, there is nothing that explains the meaning of words as well as a picture. And I take it that Michelangelo was as good as anyone can be, and did his best, and here is a picture of the deity creating Adam.
>
> If we ever saw this, we certainly wouldn't think this was the deity. The picture has to be used in an entirely different way if we are to call the man in that queer blanket 'God'. . . .[14]

In both Lecture One and Lecture Two Wittgenstein, like Kierkegaard, is concerned to contrast superstition and credulity (which often coexist with religion) from religious belief in his sense. In the first lecture, the example of *superstition* is a Catholic priest who tries to offer scientific arguments for the truths of religion. Wittgenstein's comment is:

> I would definitely call O'Hara unreasonable. I would say, if this is religious belief, then it's all superstition.
>
> But I would ridicule it not by saying it is based on insufficient evidence. I would say, here is a man who is cheating himself. You can say, this man is ridiculous because he believes, and bases it on weak reasons.[15]

In the second lecture, Wittgenstein says:

> Suppose I went to somewhere like Lourdes, in France. Suppose I went with a very credulous person. He will see blood coming out of something. He says, "There you are, Wittgenstein, how can you doubt?" I'd say, "Can it only be explained one way? Can't it be this or that?" I'd try to convince him that he'd seen nothing of any consequence. I wonder whether I would do that under all circumstances. I certainly know that I would under normal circumstances.
>
> "Oughtn't one after all to consider this?" I'd say, "come on, come on." I would treat the phenomenon in this case just

as I would treat an experiment in a laboratory which I thought badly executed.[16]

Wittgenstein is concerned to deny any continuity at all between what he considers religious belief and scientific belief. When there is a continuity, and only when there is a continuity, Wittgenstein is willing to use words like "ridiculous," "absurd," "credulous," "superstitious."

To come back now to the question of incommensurability. An example might seem to be afforded by Wittgenstein's own thought experiment at the beginning of Lecture One, of imagining two people of whom the first one says, "I believe in the Last Judgment," and the second says, "Well, I'm not so sure. Possibly." Here Wittgenstein does say, "It isn't a question of my being anywhere near him, but on an entirely different plane, which you could express by saying, 'You mean something altogether different, Wittgenstein.'"[17] Now, at the beginning of the *Philosophical Investigations* (par. 43), Wittgenstein wrote, "For a *large* class of cases — though not for all — in which we employ the word 'meaning' it can be defined thus: the meaning of a word is its use in the language." If, as is too often done, one simply ignores the qualification "though not for all," and ascribes to Wittgenstein the view that meaning can always be defined as use, then it is natural to read this "theory of meaning" back into the statement I just quoted, from the first of the "Lectures on Religious Belief." Then one would take it that when Wittgenstein insists that the religious person and the non-religious person are using words in different ways, then he literally means that the words "I believe in a Last Judgment" have a different meaning for someone who can speak of the Last Judgment as a matter of "probability" and for a religious believer. But there are at least two things wrong with this reading. First of all, Wittgenstein doesn't say this. In the notes we have of the first Lecture on Religious Belief, it is Wittgenstein's imaginary interlocutor who says, "*You* mean something altogether different, Wittgenstein." And what Wittgenstein replies to his imaginary interlocutor is, "The difference might not show up at all in any explanation of the meaning."[18]

In fine, something very lovely happens here. Wittgenstein is often charged with simple-mindedly equating use and meaning.

Yet here he imagines an interlocutor who plays the role of the stock "Wittgenstein," and proposes to say that the words "I believe in a Last Judgment" have a different meaning in the two uses. The real Wittgenstein reminds the stock "Wittgenstein" that we don't use the word "meaning" in that way. The difference in these two uses is not something that we would ordinarily call a difference in meaning.

Wittgenstein says something more about this toward the end of the same lecture. First of all, he points out that as an educated person who has read the religious classics there is a very good sense in which he knows what the religious person means, although there is another sense in which Wittgenstein is inclined to say, "I don't know whether I understand him or not."

Here is the paragraph:

If Mr. Lewy (Casimir Lewy, one of the students present at these sessions) is religious and says he believes in a Judgment Day, I won't even know whether to say I understand him or not. I've read the same things as he's read. In a most important sense, I know what he means.[19]

And Wittgenstein immediately goes on to ask,

If an atheist says, "There won't be a Judgment Day," and another person says, "There will," do they mean the same? — Not clear what the criterion of meaning the same is. They might describe the same things. You might say, this already shows that this means the same.[20]

So Wittgenstein is warning us against supposing that talk of "meaning the same" and "not meaning the same" will clarify anything here. In a perfectly ordinary sense of meaning the same, we might say that they do mean the same, although Wittgenstein is still inclined to say, "I don't even know whether I should say that I understand him or not." He might dismiss the question whether the sentence means the same, as of no help here, and thus precisely to dismiss "incommensurability" talk. That the two speakers aren't able to communicate *because* their words have different "meanings" is precisely the doctrine of incommensurability.

Another familiar move is to say that religious language is "emotive," that is, that it is used to "express attitudes." It might seem possible to read these lectures as holding some version of this doctrine, if it were not for the very end of Lecture Three. At that point Wittgenstein returns again to the question of whether he, as a nonbeliever, should say that he understands the sentences of the religious person or not. Here is the passage:

> Suppose someone, before going to China, when he might never see me again, said to me, "We might see one another after death." Would I necessarily say that I don't understand him? I might say [want to say] simply, "Yes, I *understand* him entirely."
>
> Lewy: "In this case, you might only mean that he expressed a certain attitude."
>
> I would say, "No, it isn't the same as saying I'm very fond of you, and it may not be the same as saying anything else. It says what it says. Why should you be able to substitute anything else?"
>
> Suppose I say, the man used a picture.[21]

The reply to Lewy is extremely interesting. What I take Wittgenstein to be pointing out is that there is a perfectly ordinary notion of expressing an attitude, and what he is doing is contrasting the kind of metaphysical emphasis that noncognitivists want to put on the notion of expressing an attitude with the ordinary unemphasized use of that notion. For example, if I love someone very much, I may express my love in a variety of ways. I might say, "There's absolutely no one like you." In such a case, we could say that I was expressing an attitude, my love for the person. That attitude can be expressed explicitly, by saying "I love you". However, Wittgenstein is refusing to say that language is "used to express an attitude" when there is no possibility of replacing the language in question by an explicit expression of the so-called attitude. The reason, I think, is not hard to guess. Wittgenstein refuses to make a metaphysical distinction between saying something because that is, quite literally, what one means to say; and saying something to express an attitude. As a metaphysical distinction it makes no sense at all without an appropriate metaphysical notion of a "real fact" (the sort of fact that David Lewis can "take at face value"); and that, evidently, is what Wittgenstein thinks we haven't got. In *The Claim of Reason*, Stanley Cavell suggested that

Charles Stevenson, the father of emotivism, wrote as if he had forgotten what ethical arguments sound like.[22] Wittgenstein is saying that Lewy is talking as if he had forgotten what religious language sounds like. The philosophical doctrine of noncognitivism does not help us to understand what religious discourse is really like any more than the philosophical doctrine of incommensurability does.

What then is Wittgenstein saying? I believe that Wittgenstein, in company with Kierkegaard, is saying that religious discourse can be understood in any depth only by understanding the form of life to which it belongs. What characterizes that form of life is not the expressions of belief that accompany it, but a way — a way that includes words and pictures, but is far from consisting in just words and pictures — of living one's life, of regulating all of one's decisions. Here the believer, Kierkegaard, would add something that Wittgenstein does not say, but that I think he would agree with, namely, that a person may think and say all the right words and be living a thoroughly nonreligious life. Indeed, Kierkegaard insists that a person may think she is worshipping God and really be worshipping an idol.[23] What Kierkegaard and Wittgenstein have in common is the idea that understanding the words of the religious person properly is inseparable from understanding their religious form of life,[24] and this is not a matter of "semantic theory," but a matter of understanding a human being.

The Religious Person "Uses a Picture"

Still, Wittgenstein himself does say that the religious person "uses a picture." Is this not a way of saying that religious language is noncognitive? Indeed, Yvor Smithies seems to share this worry, since he objects toward the very end of Lecture Three, "This isn't all he does — associate a use with a picture." Wittgenstein's initial reply is, "Rubbish!" Wittgenstein goes on to explain that when he says the religious man is using a picture, he does not mean by that anything that the religious person himself would not say. Here is the exchange:

> Smithies: This isn't all he does — associate a use with a
> picture.
> Wittgenstein: Rubbish! I mean, what conclusions are you

going to draw, etc. Are eyebrows going to be talked of in connection with the Eye of God?

"He could just as well have said so and so"—This remark is foreshadowed by the word "attitude." He couldn't just as well have said something else.

If I say he used a picture, I don't want to say anything he himself wouldn't say. I want to say that he draws these conclusions.

Isn't it as important as anything else what pictures he does use? Of certain pictures we might say that they might just as well be replaced by another—e.g., we could, under certain circumstances, have one projection of an ellipse drawn instead of another.

He *may* say: I would have been prepared to use another picture—it would have the same effect. . . .

The whole *weight* may be in the picture. . . . When I say he is using a picture, I am making a *grammatical* remark. What I say can only be verified by the consequences he does or does not draw.

If Smithies disagrees, I don't take notice of this disagreement.

All I wished to characterize was the consequences he wished to draw. If I wished to say anything more, I was merely being philosophically arrogant.[25]

"All I wished to characterize was the consequences he wished to draw. If I wished to say anything more, I was merely being philosophically arrogant." This has to be one of the most impressive remarks a great philosopher has ever made in a discussion! Wittgenstein is saying here that to say the religious person is using a picture is simply to describe what we can in fact observe. Religious people do employ pictures, and they draw certain consequences from them, but not the same consequences that we draw when we use similar pictures in other contexts. If I speak of my friend as having an eye, then normally I am prepared to say that he has an eyebrow; but when I speak of the Eye of God being upon me, I am not prepared to speak of the eyebrow of God. The impressive thing here is not what Wittgenstein says, but the limit he places on his own observation. Pictures are important in life. The whole weight of a form of life may lie in the pictures that

that form of life uses. In his own notes, some of which are re-published in the collection *Culture and Value*, Wittgenstein writes: "It is true that we can compare a picture that is firmly rooted in us to a superstition, but it is equally true that we *always* eventually have to reach some firm ground, either a picture or something else, so that a picture which is at the root of all our thinking is to be respected, and not treated as a superstition."[26]

In passing, I should like to say that these remarks seem to go totally against the idea that Wittgenstein was against pictures as such. When Wittgenstein attacks philosophers for being in the grip of a picture, the usual reading of this is that Wittgenstein opposed pictures, that pictures are bad. But Wittgenstein in his lectures during the 1930s repeatedly praises pictures in two ways.[27] First, he praises them as good ways of explaining the meaning of words. We had an example of this already in Lecture One. Second, he speaks of pictures as having "weight," or of pictures being such that one's life can depend on them. Evidently, then, if certain philosophers are attacked by Wittgenstein for being in the grip of a picture, his reason is not that pictures are bad, but that certain pictures are bad. Wittgenstein believes that there are pictures that should not "grip" one, presumably because they lack any significant "weight," because they are not the sort of pictures on which anyone's life can "depend."[28]

To return to religious language, even though Wittgenstein here does not say that religious language is noncognitive, because he doesn't "want to say anything that [the religious person] wouldn't say," he has by implication, at least, said that it is noncognitive. One might suggest that this is what Smithies was sensitive to and what Wittgenstein refused "to take notice of."

Wittgenstein on Reference

But what can *noncognitive* come to when one suggests that "religious language is noncognitive"? The traditional realist way to spell out this suggestion would be to say that while terms like "my brother" and "America" and "The Arc de Triomphe" all refer, Wittgenstein may be suggesting that words used in religious contexts do not refer. Isn't Wittgenstein hinting that when one speaks of the Eye of God one is *only* using a picture, that is to say, one isn't referring to anything? Isn't he hinting that when one speaks of the Last Judgment one is *only* using a picture, that is, one isn't referring to anything?

Strangely enough, Wittgenstein interrupts Lecture Three to talk about the phenomenon of a thought's being about "my brother in America." This is a case of what Husserl called "intentionality." Wittgenstein also uses the term "reference." He speaks of the thought as being "about" his brother in America, and also about sentences and words as "referring" or "designating." There is no indication at all in these notes as to why Wittgenstein interrupted a lecture on religious belief to discuss this subject. The notes that we have on Lecture Three run from page 65 to page 72 of the volume edited by Cyril Barrett, and almost three full pages (66 to 68) are occupied by this discussion of reference. The discussion is set off by white spaces before and after, so the editors themselves evidently recognized this as some kind of a digression.

Moreover, the textual evidence suggests a digression. What precedes the digression is a question about two phrases, "ceasing to exist" and "being a disembodied spirit." Wittgenstein says, "When I say this, I think of myself having a certain set of experiences. What is it like to think of this?" And Wittgenstein comes back to this question after the digression on reference. But no examples from either religious language or from spiritualism (which Wittgenstein contrasts with religion) occur in the digression on reference. The only example used in that digression is thinking of Wittgenstein's "brother in America." Yet I don't think this "digression" can possibly be an accident. It speaks to just the fear that I suggested may lie behind Smithies's remark, the fear that Wittgenstein is at least hinting at a fundamental difference between religious language and nonreligious language; namely, that religious language does not refer, or is not "about" anything. The worry is that in ordinary language we have pictures and uses of pictures and something beyond the words and pictures. In religious language, on the other hand, we have only pictures and words and uses of the pictures and words.

I suggest that when Wittgenstein said "Rubbish!" in response to Smithies's remark, and then hastily added that he only meant to make a "grammatical" remark, Wittgenstein's initial impatience is accounted for by his belief that he had at least implicitly dealt with the issue Smithies was raising. But how had he dealt with it?

The first point that Wittgenstein makes is one that sounds odd today when there are so many discussions of "causal theories of reference." Wittgenstein is struck by the fact that he can think of his brother in America even though there is no causal interaction between him and his brother taking place now. Indeed, Wittgenstein assumes that we don't even think of reference as a causal relation. Our natural temptation is to think that the intentionality of our words is something given in the experience of thought itself. "If you're asked, how do you know that it is a thought of such and such, the thought that immediately comes to your mind is that of a shadow, a picture. You don't think of a causal relation. The kind of relation you think of is best expressed by 'picture,' 'shadow,' etc."[29] And Wittgenstein goes on to talk in a way familiar to readers of the *Investigations* about the way in which we simultaneously tend to think of thoughts as mental pictures and to ascribe to them powers that no actual picture could possibly have.

> The word "picture" is even quite all right. In many cases, it is even in the most ordinary sense a picture. You might translate my very words into a picture.[30] But the point is, suppose you do this. How do I know it is my brother in America? Who says it is him — unless it is here ordinary similarity?
>
> What is the connection between these words or anything substitutable for them with my brother in America?
>
> The first idea you have is that you are looking at your own thought and are absolutely sure that it is a thought that so and so. You are looking at some mental phenomenon, and you say to yourself, obviously this is a thought of my brother in America. It seems to be a super-picture. It seems with thought that there is no doubt whatever. With a picture it still depends on the method of projection, whereas here it seems that you get rid of the projecting relation and are absolutely certain that this is a thought of that.[31]

Now the idea that intentionality is simultaneously something given in experience and yet a relation to something external to the experience is certainly a muddle; Wittgenstein is right about that. But why does he dismiss thinking of reference as a causal connection so quickly?

There is a way of making the problem clear. It goes back to Frege and even back to Kant. The sentence "The cat is on the mat" consists of exactly the same words as the mere list, "the," "cat," "is," "on," "the," "mat." Yet the sentence has a truth value, in an appropriate situation, while the list has no truth value. What constitutes the difference between a sentence and a list? The phrase "the first baby born after the year 3000" has a referent, while the list consisting of those words in that order does not refer to anything. Again, what constitutes the difference? In Kant's terminology, a judgment is not just a series of representations but a "synthesis" of those representations. It was just this problem that led Frege to give priority to sentence meaning over word meaning in his theorizing about language.

The answer to this problem is obvious after Wittgenstein. A sentence can have a truth value or a complex phrase can have reference, whereas a mere list of words has neither truth value nor reference, because we *use* sentences and complex phrases in very different ways from the ways in which we use mere lists. But this observation totally undercuts the idea of a mere causal theory of reference. Referring, I repeat, is using words in a certain way. It may well be that a certain referring use of some words would be impossible if we were not causally connected to the kinds of things referred to. Indeed, I believe that this is the case. But that is to say that there are causal constraints on reference, not that the referring *is* the causal connection. No matter how the word *cat* is causally connected to the world, if I say "cat, cat, cat, cat, cat . . ." a hundred times, I am not referring to cats, whereas if I use the word *cat* in certain ways, I am referring to cats.

In the digression on reference I described, Wittgenstein speaks of what I am calling a referring use of language as "technique." He suggests here that the illusion of intrinsic intentionality, that reference is a mysterious something that exists while we think and about which nothing can be said, is due to the fact that we only pay attention to the mental experience and not to the technique of using the word:

> Is thinking something going on at the particular time, or is it something spread over the words? It comes in a flash. Always?— It sometimes does come in a flash, although this may be all sorts of different things.

If it does refer to a technique, then it can't be enough in certain cases to explain what you mean in a few words, because there is something which might be thought to be in conflict with the idea going on from 7 to 75, namely, the practice of using it.

When we talked about so and so as an "automaton," the stronghold of that view was due to the idea that you could say, "Well, I know what I mean," as though you were looking at something that were happening while you said the thing, entirely independent of what came before and after the application of the phrase. It looked as if you could talk of understanding a word without any reference to the technique of its usage. It looked as though Smithies said he could understand the sentence, and we then had nothing to say.[32]

At one time, I myself had the hope that what Wittgenstein refers to as the use of words could be completely surveyed and analyzed in a functionalist way. I had hoped that all the various referring uses of words could all be neatly organized and depicted by something like a super computer program. In my *Representation and Reality*, I explained my reasons for thinking it overwhelmingly likely that this cannot be done. But if we cannot survey all the referring uses of words, then there is a sense in which we don't have a *theory* of "the nature of reference" at all, not even if we succeeded in showing that our words are causally attached to what they refer to in certain ways. If we cannot give some kind of a scientific theory of the referring uses of our words, then how are we to look at reference?

In *Philosophical Investigations* Wittgenstein attacks the idea that one can only use a word if one possesses some kind of necessary and sufficient condition for its application. He uses the word *game* as an example, and he says that in the case of that word we don't have a necessary and sufficient condition. We have paradigms of different kinds, and we extend the word *game* to new cases because they strike us as similar to cases in which we have used it before. He speaks of games as forming a family, of games as having a family resemblance, and he uses the metaphor of a rope. The fibers of the rope are similarities, but there is no fiber running the length of the whole rope. There are similarities between one game and another, but there is no one similarity between all games.

While the notion of a family resemblance word has become a commonplace, many people miss Wittgenstein's point. As Rush Rhees emphasized a long time ago, Wittgenstein was not just making a low-level empirical observation to the effect that in addition to words like *scarlet*, which apply to things all of which are similar in a particular respect, there are words like *game* which apply to things which are not all similar in some one respect.[33] No. Wittgenstein was primarily thinking not of words like *game* but of words like *language* and *reference*. It is precisely the big philosophical notions to which Wittgenstein wishes to apply the notion of a family resemblance. On Rush Rhees's reading, what Wittgenstein is telling us is that referring uses don't have an "essence." There isn't some one thing which can be called "referring." There are overlapping similarities between one sort of referring and the next, and that is all. This is why, for example, Wittgenstein is not puzzled, as many philosophers are, about how we can "refer" to abstract entities. After all, we are not causally attached to the number *three*, so how can we refer to it? Indeed, do we know that there is such an object at all? For Wittgenstein the fact is that the use of number words is simply a different use from the use of words like *cow*. Start calling *three* an "object" or an "abstract entity" and look at the way number words are used, is his advice.

The relevance of this to Wittgenstein's "Lectures on Religious Belief" is as follows. I have suggested that Wittgenstein would not have regarded talk of incommensurability as helpful, and would not have regarded talk of certain discourses' being "cognitive" and other discourses' being "noncognitive" as helpful. I also suggest that he would not have regarded the question as to whether religious language *refers* as helpful either. He speaks of a "muddle." The use of religious language is both like and unlike ordinary uses of language to refer; but to ask whether it is "really" reference or "not really" reference is to be in a muddle. There is no essence of reference. Religious thinkers will be the first to tell you that when they refer to God, their "referring use" is quite unlike the referring use of "his brother in America."[34] In short, Wittgenstein is telling you what *isn't* the way to understand religious language. The way to understand religious language is *not* to try to apply some metaphysical classification of possible forms of discourse.

NOTES

1. See Ludwig Wittgenstein, *Lectures and Conversations on Aesthetics, Psychology, and Religious Belief*, ed. Cyril Barrett (Berkeley, Calif.: University of California Press, 1966.

2. Ibid., p. 53.

3. Ibid.

4. Ibid.

5. Ibid., p. 54.

6. Wittgenstein also said in the first lecture, "It has been said a thousand times, and by intelligent people, that indubitability is not enough in this case [Christianity]. Even if there is as much evidence as for Napoleon. Because the indubitability wouldn't be enough to make me change my whole life. It doesn't rest on a historic basis (in the sense that the ordinary belief in historic facts could serve as a foundation)" (ibid., p. 57). Compare this with what Soren Kierkegaard said about the historical argument in the *Concluding Unscientific Postscript* (Princeton, N.J.: Princeton University Press, 1941), pp. 25–48. When he cites "intelligent people" is he speaking of Kierkegaard?

7. Kierkegaard, *Concluding Unscientific Postscript*, p. 53.

8. Wittgenstein, *Lectures and Conversations on Aesthetics, Psychology, and Religious Belief*, p. 55.

9. Ibid.

10. Ibid., p. 56.

11. The notes were taken by three people, and the editor says that they agreed very closely with one another.

12. Ibid., p. 55.

13. Ibid., p. 63.

14. Ibid.

15. Ibid., p. 59.

16. Ibid., pp. 60–61.

17. Ibid., p. 53.

18. Ibid.

19. Ibid., p. 58.

20. Ibid.

21. Ibid., p. 70.

22. Stanley Cavell, *The Claim of Reason* (New York: Oxford University Press, 1979), pp. 247–91.

23. I suspect that this is one of the reasons that Kierkegaard is so much hated by fundamentalists. For Kierkegaard an authentically religious form of life is characterized by a constant concern that one not replace the idea of God with a narcissistic creation of one's own; and this

concern expresses itself in uncertainty as much as in certainty. For Kierke-gaard, to be absolutely sure one is "born again" is a sign that one is lost.

24. I want to acknowledge that I have been very much aided in arriving at this understanding of Kierkegaard by Stanley Cavell's essay "Existentialism and Analytical Philosophy," in his *Themes out of School* (Berkeley, Calif.: North Point Press, 1984), and also by a long study of James Conant's, "Kierkegaard, Wittgenstein, and Nonsense," in *Pursuits of Reason, Essays Presented to Stanley Cavell*, ed. T. Cohen, P. Guyer, and H. Putnam (Lubbock, Tex.: Texas Tech University Press, forthcom-ing), in which he compares the exegetical difficulties in reading Wittgen-stein's *Tractatus* and those we face in reading Kierkegaard's *Concluding Unscientific Postscript*. I do not, of course, suggest that either Cavell or Conant would necessarily agree with the formulations here.

25. Wittgenstein, *Lectures and Conversations on Aesthetics, Psy-chology, and Religious Belief*, pp. 71–72.

26. Ludwig Wittgenstein, *Culture and Value* (Chicago: University of Chicago Press, 1980), p. 83.

27. See, for example, lecture 25 in Ludwig Wittgenstein, *Lectures on the Foundations of Mathematics*, ed. Cora Diamond (Ithaca, N.Y.: Cornell University Press, 1976).

28. James Conant has suggested to me that one should also con-sider the metaphor of *gripping* involved in "being in the grip of a pic-ture." The suggestion is that perhaps philosophical pictures constrain one, rather than liberating one.

29. Wittgenstein, *Lectures and Conversations on Aesthetics, Psy-chology, and Religious Belief*, p. 66.

30. Again we note that Wittgenstein has no hostility to pictures as such, or to the idea of connecting words with pictures.

31. Wittgenstein, *Lectures and Conversations on Aesthetics, Psy-chology, and Religious Belief*, p. 67.

32. Ibid., p. 68.

33. See his review of George Pitcher's book, *The Philosophy of Witt-genstein*, in Rush Rhees, *Discussions of Wittgenstein* (London: Routledge & Kegan Paul, 1970), ch. 4, pp. 37–54.

34. In this connection, see the chapter on negative theology in Ken-neth Seeskin, *Jewish Philosophy in a Secular Age* (Albany, N.Y.: State University of New York Press, 1990).

4

Selfhood, Nature, and Society: Ernest Hocking's Metaphysics of Community

LEROY S. ROUNER

TO BE IN COMMUNITY WITH OURSELVES, others, and the natural world around us is to be at home in those worlds. The most primal and instinctive sense of being at home comes to most of us through the natural bonds of blood, region, language, caste or class, and religion, which are the bonds of traditional and tribal cultures. They are not as strong with us mobile, modern people who live most of our lives in urban industrial centers as they are with Indian villagers, Southeast Asian peasants, and African tribespeople, but we feel their power nevertheless.

Beyond the rational specifics of economy and political ideology, there is in us all, I suggest, a visceral instinct which makes us gravitate toward our own kind and fear the stranger. We still feel the old bonds and they give us what we now call our roots. To be part of this family, however contentious; to be familiar with this place of childhood memory; to know this language's local accent and intimate meanings; to have a place, however low, in this community; and to share with others the celebration of this religious belief and commitment, in which the deepest in us meets the deepest in our community — this is what it means to be at home.

Those whom we perceive to be different from us are outsiders, aliens, strangers. We may be fascinated by them and occasionally even join forces with them, but when it is them against us — Protestants against Catholics in Ireland, Tamils against Sinhalese in Sri Lanka, Arabs against Israelis in the Middle East — what is at stake for us is deeper than economic self-interest or even ideological commitment. What is threatened is our sense of being at home in our world. And our need to be at home is deep and powerful.

The problem which this raises for us is the pluralism of the coming world civilization. These *others* are now not only our neighbors in the global village but our partners in the task of human survival. My enthusiasm for this situation is qualified. I like novelty, occasional change, and people who are different from me, but our current cultural pluralism is a thunderstorm, a flood, a raging fire. There is no way that any one person can encompass it all or make sense of it all, or even survive it all if we were honestly open to its total impact. Pluralism makes us all bobbing corks on its cultural ocean, in the midst of a typhoon. But here we are, and the only serious question is how we are to ride out the storm.

Philosophy seems like a weak vehicle for that ride, especially when compared to the thick, strong bonds of our natural identities. But it provides a universality which natural bonds do not, and even a weak conception of universality may help. If philosophy can provide some thin, overarching, vague rationale for who we are, and how we can find common ground with these strangers who are now our neighbors and partners, that is no small service. That was the service which Ernest Hocking's metaphysics intended to provide. His metaphysics then became the superstructure upon which his philosophies of history, religion, and world culture were built.

He begins with the three fundamental elements in human experience: ourselves, other selves, and physical nature. Everything in experience is an I, a Thou, or an It. As he read the story of modern philosophy since Descartes, he saw that the philosophical connections among these three had been severed. The most serious aspect of that fragmentation of experience was the isolation of one self from another. Modern philosophy had robbed us of our ability to explain how we know the other person to be a mind like our own. Social knowledge had been reduced to behaviorism. We know other persons only through what their bodies do. We have no direct access to the mind, or spirit, or soul of the other. Hence the characteristic spiritual affliction of modernity is loneliness; and solipsism (the view that we can know only the internal states of our own minds), the metaphysics of loneliness, became for Hocking the contemporary philosophical problem most in need of solution.

The Idea of a Purposeless Nature

The medieval interpreters of Aristotle integrated the human philosophical desire for understanding the "reasons why" (*to dioti*) things are as they are with the divine love which is God's will that things should be the way they are. Medieval science was therefore human wisdom conjoined with divine truth. In the Elizabethan period, however, there was a major shift in the understanding of science, popularized by Francis Bacon, and his insistence that the aim of science is useful knowledge. Knowledge now becomes power *over* the forces of physical nature. As Bacon put it so eloquently,

> I will give thee the greatest jewel I have. For I will impart to thee, for the love of God and men, a relation of the true state of Salomon's House. . . . The end of our foundation is the knowledge of causes and secret motions of things, and the enlarging of the bounds of human empire, to effecting of all things possible.[1]

For the Greeks, science was elegant explanation, a fit pursuit of lofty minds for whom affluence had granted leisure to reflect on principles of understanding. For medieval Christianity, science was faithful uncovering of the ways in which God effected God's will in the world. But for Bacon and his successors science explored the laws of matter in motion in order to command nature. The purpose of scientific study is "to turn heaven and earth to the use and welfare of mankind."[2] This was in sharp contrast to the medieval view of science, inherited from Aristotle. For Aristotle, a theory of knowledge was precisely a theory of the world's intelligibility, in which the power of the knower to know a thing joined with the power of the thing to be known.

Notable here is Aristotle's understanding of nature. Everything has a material cause, the stuff of which it is made; an efficient cause, the process whereby it comes to be; a formal cause, the particular kind which makes it this sort of thing rather than that sort; and a final cause, which is Aristotle's name for the purpose of a thing. The purpose of a maple tree, for example, is to be a real, or perfected, maple. In its career from seed to sapling the maple tree is aiming at something. Just as a growing boy is aiming at manhood, so a growing sapling is aiming at becoming a properly full-grown tree.

This notion that the natural world has purpose of some sort is part of Aristotle's view of the world as intelligible, and intelligibility is not radically different for natural things and for persons. Natural objects are not "objects" or "things" in the modern sense because they have an active role to play in the knowing process. For Aristotle a yellow wall has the power to be seen as yellow. We do not have the power to know it apart from its power to be known. So knowing something is not solely the function of an individual mind. It is a natural function which takes place in an intelligible world, and it requires both the power of the individual knower to know a thing and the power of the thing itself to be known.

In contrast, modern theories of knowledge, from Bacon and Descartes to Kant, think of knowledge as an event taking place within an individual mind, made possible by the power of the individual mind to know. This view understands nature primarily in terms of Aristotle's material and efficient causes. His formal cause — the natural kind of thing which this particular thing is — is no longer inherent in the thing itself, or derived from participation in some Platonic idea. Formal cause is now only the way we understand it and talk about it, and the name we arbitrarily decide to give it. Formal cause becomes a function of signs and symbols of understanding in the mind, rather than the inherent intelligibility of the thing in and of itself. And final cause is removed from metaphysical analysis altogether. We no longer speak of a tree as having any natural purpose.

The Divorce between Nature and Mind

Building on the view that all knowledge is grounded in the absolutely certain and immediate knowledge which one has of one's own mind, Descartes admits that our knowledge of physical nature, and our knowledge of other minds than our own, becomes problematic. Aristotle's natural realism celebrated a sunny and untroubled confidence that the world is a coherent whole in which

my mind, other minds, and physical nature are integrated by a
Nous (world mind) which, while primarily evident in the work-
ings of your mind and mine, is also evident in the structure and
purposive operations of physical nature. Hence the entire experienced world is illumined with the light of intelligibility. In such
a world human minds are not radically separated from nature,
nor is my mind fundamentally at a loss to explain its instinctive
assurance that you, who are distinct from me, also have a mind
of your own.

With the Cartesian shift, however, illumination no longer
floods the world. The light of reason illuminates the inwardness
of the individual mind. "Cogito ergo sum" (I think; therefore I
am). The mind of my neighbor, however, although not quite covered
with darkness, is, to me, a twilight of confusion. We all know perfectly well that the neighbor has a mind precisely like our own,
but our "other minds problem" expresses our inability to explain
to ourselves how we know this. The natural world, on the other
hand, is not in twilight; it is cast into an epistemological outer
darkness. To define a physical object simply as something that takes
up space, a *res extensa*, is to announce a mystery. We know that
there is something out there, and we know how it appears to us,
but we cannot know what it is in itself.

Aristotle and the medievals knew the "treeness" of the tree
from the inside, so to speak, because they knew its purpose in being that kind of tree. The implications of the Cartesian view were
later made specific by Kant, when he pointed out that all knowledge begins with the reality of the individual knower. He observes,
irrefutably, that I can only know what I know. All that I know
is logically preceded by the realization that I am knowing it. This
"I think" must be presupposed in any knowledge claim by any mind.
Any particular act of knowing is thus radically relativized. What
the object may be in and for itself must always be unknown to
me. For the modern mind, therefore, knowledge of nature became
knowledge from the "outside."

The individualization of the knowing process aggrandized the
power of the individual mind as the sole active agent in the knowing process. Our perceptions grasp and shape bits and pieces of
experience from which our concepts construct a world. We are the
creators of our world. Perception is now a raid on the unknow-

able, a bequeathing of status and reality on that which, apart from the mind's gracious attention, must remain dark and dumb. Aristotle's nature, enlivened by the purposive presence of the world Mind or *Nous*, here becomes shrouded and alien.

Aristotle's world, and the medieval world which built on it, was a metaphysical community. Its lines of connection made intelligible the relations among individuals, their fellows, and the natural world which was their setting. In breaking down our understanding of these relations, modernity has sacrificed that visceral sense of community which lets us feel at home in our experienced world of ourselves, others, and nature. It was this metaphysical community which Hocking sought to restore.

He was not willing to go back to Aristotle or the medievals, however, because he believed that something significant had been achieved in the Cartesian shift which he wanted to perserve. That achievement was precisely the distinction between the world of mind, *res cogitans*, and the world of matter, *res extensa*. This distinction is true to our experience — people are different from trees or rocks — and it opens up the creative possibilities of modern science.

It is currently popular to criticize dualisms of all sorts in the name of integrated holisms, but Hocking was persuaded that dualism was a problem that each culture needed to work through. When the Chinese neo-Confucian scholar Hu Shin announced proudly that China had had no Descartes, Hocking responded that that was part of their problem and had prevented them from creative engagement with the possibilities of modernity. Modern life requires a purposeless nature, he believed, and he insisted that that purposelessness had been given to us for a purpose: the creative purposes of modern science and technology. Even the kind of ecology we could all be happy with would require that we dam *some* rivers and fell *some* trees, and we are not morally free to do that if nature has purposes with which we are interfering. Perhaps even more to the point are those quantum leaps in modern medicine which have made a better and longer life possible for increasing numbers of people, because we have learned how to subdue natural viruses and control them.

His primary commitment was to fashion a metaphysics which would be true to our experience. The problem is that our experience is not unified in a simple way. His colleague Whitehead had a nice way of putting it. He remarked that "sometimes I think that I am in the world; and sometimes I think that the world is in me." In other words, we have two radically different kinds of experience of ourselves in our world.

One he called natural realism. The world was here before we entered it and will be here after we leave it, and we know ourselves now to be in that world. The other he called subjective idealism. The world I know is always, inescapably, the world as known to me. Natural objects, for example, are known to me only through sense perception, and my knowledge of these objects is a conception which lives in my head. That world is *in* me.

Hocking wanted to do justice to both these experiences, and his metaphysics is therefore dialectical, in a manner which distinguishes his view from that of his teachers, Josiah Royce and William James. James's pragmatic and pluralistic philosophy of radical empiricism understood reality as a forward flow of "pure experience," a view which has since endeared him to Buddhists, Whiteheadians, and other "go-with-the-flow" philosophers. Royce's metaphysics of the Absolute, on the other hand, had trouble moving at all. His metaphysics never entirely escaped Ralph Barton Perry's criticism that he was proposing a static "block universe," because the really Real in Royce's world is an unchanging transcendental idea.

Hocking thought reality moves, but not in a forward flow. It zigs and zags. Reality, he thought, is like the learning process, and in Hocking's system even God learns, because God does not know the future, and the unfolding future of free human activity is endlessly instructive to the mind of God. Learning is the process whereby we get an idea about something, only to have it countered by a different idea, which we then incorporate into our original understanding, for a better idea of the thing. As in Hegel, the meeting of thesis and antithesis produces a synthesis. The question is then: What kind of synthesis can resolve the crisis in our experience between the natural realism of our conviction that we are in the world, and the subjective idealism of our reflection that our experienced world is really in us?

In search of a solution, Hocking went back to Descartes, whose famous "Cogito ergo sum" (I think; therefore I am) seemed to him only half right. He agreed with Descartes that immediate knowledge of our own minds is the certitude which makes philosophy possible in the first place. The reality of a thought necessarily requires the reality of a thinker. But, as it stands, the statement doesn't really make any sense, because it is impossible simply to think. You have to think *something*. So the objects of physical nature, the things I think about, are *necessary* for thought.

That's the key point. I couldn't think unless I had something to think about. It is nature which lends clarity, pungency, definition, specificity, to thought. In that sense, natural objects, as the content of mind, are mind-stuff. And since it is nature which thus makes mind possible, and gives us the objects which become the content of mind, Hocking goes on to note that nature is therefore "creative of mind in me."

That may sound animistic, but at least it was not simply speculative. Hocking used to say that metaphysics is an "out-of-doors" business. Virtually all the major turning points in his philosophical development involved specific experiences which took place out-of-doors. The crucial one here is described in a key passage of *The Meaning of God in Human Experience*.[3] He says, in effect, Why is it that when I look at you I see only your exterior, your body, the forehead which encases your mind; and never the real you? This exterior wall of your presence is only a movable part of my world, and I am also only a wall, a facade, to you. Your mind is lurking there, behind your forehead, "fraternizing with chemical processes," as he can't resist saying. But then he asks himself, Is that really where *my* mind is? Well, no. When, with Descartes, he said that the mind, which is the self, is necessarily presupposed by any thought that that mind may have, he wasn't talking about chemical processes gurgling away back there in the brain. He notes that he doesn't have any experience of chemical brain processes. His experience of his mind is purely an experience of its content. Here Hocking agreed with James. Consciousness, as some sort of separate substance, doesn't exist; or at least, we don't have any distinguishable experience of it as existing apart from the content of consciousness. *My* mind *is* its content. It is what I am thinking *about*. And if your mind is also its content, then we both share the same content insofar as we share the same experienced world.

We sit here, out of doors, looking at the same mountain, and that mountain is the common content of our common mind. Yes, you see it from a slightly different angle, and you don't feel about it quite the same way I feel about it. Your mountain is not quite the same as my mountain, because you are you and I am me — and *vive la difference*! Otherwise Sameness would be King and we would all die of boredom. But the major characteristic of this particular mountain is the common reality which you and I absorb in our own slightly different ways, and that objective point of departure is the same for all observers. If we didn't have these objects in common we would all be crazy and life would be impossible.

So nature is known as the content of other minds. But what if there is no one else sitting there with us looking at the mountain? Do we still experience the mountain as "creative of mind in me?" Yes, we are still persuaded of its objectivity. Scientific objectivity, he notes, is established by the confirmation of another observer. We know that we are seeing something real when another observer says that he or she also sees the same thing. And that is the way we experience the mountain, even when there is no other mind immediately present to view it with us. We know it as objective, that is, as known by other minds.

But what sort of other mind could confirm that objective reality? Our minds are passive. We must take the world as it is given to us. But Hocking finds nature as "creative of mind" in him. That is to say, nature is the stuff of an active mind, not one that knows passively and empirically, one which comes and goes from any particular scene as our minds must do. Nature is the stuff of an active mind which does *not* come and go but is present always and everywhere in the mind-creating work which is nature presenting itself to our thought.

Once again, this notion of all-encompassing thought is not speculative. We have an experience of this thought in the form of an idea of the Whole. It is difficult to establish the significance of this Whole idea, because it is not the specific content of our ideas; it is the unspecific background which makes those ideas possible. The Whole idea is not what we are thinking *about*; it is the basic idea we are thinking *with*. In order to make his point he casts about for the simplest and most unlikely example. Well, what about hats? With what idea do I think *hat*? What intellectual framework gives meaning to my notion of a hat?

With the hat-idea, to be sure. Yes, but is the clothing-idea unconcerned?— or the city-street-idea? or the civilized-society-extraordinary-requirements idea? or the man-and-woman-idea? or the whole mass of aesthetic notions, and political, historical, even religious opinions? With all these, and with all other ideas summing themselves up currently in my whole-idea, hat is thought.[4]

The dialectic of our experience of nature thus begins with the thesis of natural realism and is countered by the antithesis of subjective idealism. The synthesis of these two notions is that nature is the realm of other mind. The new exploration begins with this thesis of nature as realm of other mind and is countered with the notion of our own empirical minds which must know nature passively, and only occasionally. The synthesis in this second movement of the dialectic is of a mind which knows actively, creating mind in us, an absolute mind which does not come and go. This mind is experienced by us as that Whole idea which we know prior to any specific content of natural objects, and which is the possibility of our having a coherent context for any specific knowledge. This idea of the Whole or Absolute is part of what we mean by God, and it is this idea which reestablishes our community with nature and with our neighbors.

> As simply as Nature presents itself as objective, just so simply and directly is the Other Mind present to me in that objectivity, as its actual meaning. I do not first know my physical world as a world of *objects* and then as a world of *shared* objects: it is through a prior recognition of the presence of Other Mind that my physical experience acquires objectivity at all. The objectivity of Nature is its community, not two facts but one; but the *whole* truth of this one fact (the whole I do not see unless I note what I am thinking *with*) — the whole of this fact is community.[5]

Conclusion

In *The Rise of American Philosophy* Bruce Kuklick concludes his chapter on Hocking with the comment that, since Hocking disputed Royce over the issue of solipsism, he did not accept Royce's view that other selves were social constructs. Clearly Hocking "desired to distinguish his idealism by making selfhood social. Here, however, he disappointed. He wrote that God's creations were not apart from God, that God 'included' other selves and their objects. What was the relation, then, between God, the world, and other selves? Hocking wanted to avoid absolute solipsism, but he never clarified his position."[6]

I agree with Kuklick that Hocking needed to write a systematic metaphysics in order to clarify his position. The Gifford Lectures on "Fact and Destiny" were to have been his "duty book" (as Whitehead called *Process and Reality*, his own systematic metaphysics), but he never published them. He did some new work on the philosophy of selfhood on the basis of field theory, and the idea of the self as "a field of fields" became important enough that a revised sketch of his unfinished metaphysics was entitled "Fact, Field, and Destiny."

On the other hand, Kuklick's criticism doesn't focus on the crucial unfinished issue. That issue is whether or not Hocking can make his qualified metaphysical dualism coherent. The problem is not that God "includes" the creation. Of course God does, in some sense, "include" the created order of self, nature, and society. That idea is virtually inescapable in any Christian philosophy where God is creator, sustainer, and redeemer of the world. Nor is the problem that creation is not "apart from" God, another way of putting the same idea. The issue is not that Hocking put his position this way; it is that he did not fully spell out what "include" and "not apart from" were to mean in his dialectical system.

Some things can be said about his intention in this regard. Charles Hartshorne once admitted that he could not see the difference between Hocking and Berkeley, but it is clear at least that Hocking did not intend Berkeley's subjective idealism and its view that the natural object is an idea in the mind of God. Nor would Hocking have been happy with my colleague John Findlay's notion that the natural particular is an "instantiation" of a transcendental idea. Hocking was a neo-Hegelian, not a Neoplatonist — a distinction which Findlay would not have admitted but which seems significant to me.

For Plato, dialectic is a method of knowing in our world of phenomena. As in Socrates' illustration of "the divided line" in the *Republic*, dialectic functions only on the phenomenal side of the line, not in the realm of the transcendent ideas. Dialectic leads you to a "synoptic intuition" (Windelband) of the ultimate nature of things, the idea of the Good. That ultimacy is not, itself, dialectical. But for Hocking, dialectic characterizes the entire nature of things, the world of the transcendent as well as the world of natural phenomena. Even God is a learner. As in Hartshorne's dipolar theism, Hocking's God is, in one sense, unfinished, because God cannot know the future, the future not yet being available as an object of thought. Hocking loved to say, "God does not know what I am going to do tomorrow."

Hocking intended to do justice to the contradictory nature of experience with a view of reality in which God both includes and is in some sense distinct from the world, and in which we are both free from and inextricably bound to God. He intended to defend the realism of objective physical nature and its purposelessness, and to say that its purposelessness had been given to us for a purpose. Dialectic does not dissolve objectivity into subjectivity. It announces instead that physical nature is both fact and idea; that selves are both individuals and inextricably bound in community; that even God is both Whole and unfinished.

Had Charles Peirce lived to befriend Hocking the way he befriended Royce, he might well have given him the same advice: that his system needed logical tightening. Some revision or elaboration of the principle of noncontradiction is required in order to make dialectic more coherent. But I suspect that he never wrote his "duty book" because he never believed it possible to provide a logical argument which would be philosophically compelling. What he sought was a system which would be experientially appealing. What he wanted to say was, "This is my experience. Is it yours also? Does it have something of our common humanity in it?"

I find his philosophy successful in those terms. My experience is complex, not simple; ambivalent, not smoothly forward-moving. My life does not "go with the flow"; it bobs and weaves. I yearn for a sense of community with my neighbors and with nature, and I accept the fact that natural bonds of blood, region, language, caste or class, and religion are no longer viable in the radical pluralism of the coming world civilization.

Can the thin gruel of philosophy substitute for the thick bonds of natural identity? No. We are always going to love and die for our parents and our children before we take on the universal community of the coming world civilization. But while philosophy may be thin gruel, it is better than some unreflective ideology, which is its only competitor in providing a posttraditional sense of who we are and what we are supposed to be doing in the modern world. If we only cling to our natural blood relations, we are going to be lemmings, rushing toward the cliff, and that is not a great way to go.

If there is to be a human future, we need to be guided by some vague, general, inclusive notion of who we are and what we are supposed to be about. And for that task, I know no better guide than Ernest Hocking.

NOTES

1. Francis Bacon, *Novum Organum* 1.14.
2. Ibid.
3. William Ernest Hocking, *The Meaning of God in Human Experience* (New Haven, Conn.: Yale University Press, 1912), pp. 265–66.
4. Ibid., p. 131.
5. Ibid., pp. 288–89.
6. Bruce Kuklick, *The Rise of American Philosophy* (New Haven, Conn.: Yale University Press, 1977), p. 489. His reference is to Hocking, *The Meaning of God in Human Experience*, p. 298.

PART II

Community
in
Various Cultures

5

Global Japan: Internationalism in the Intimate Community

MERRY I. WHITE

JAPAN'S NUMBER ONE *DOMESTIC* ISSUE TODAY is internationalization.

How can that be? Japan seems already well international-ized: three Japanese banks last month loaned Massachusetts 1.2 billion dollars. Japanese concerns have bought control of Rocke-feller Center, much of downtown Los Angeles, and a lot of Wai-kiki. The Japanese are at the forefront of foreign involvement in the Common Market and are moving rapidly into eastern Europe as well. Japan seems not only internationalized but on its way to global dominance. There are paradoxes, however, which surround Japan's overseas excursions. In particular, the social and cultural meanings of community as understood and practiced in Japan seem to be at odds with the internationalization of Japan.

Viewed from Japan, the *sushi*-ization of our world has a rather different feel. From this perspective, Japan is a reluctant member of the modern global community.

Several years ago I was a participant in a conference on the nature of *Japan*, what's called *nihonjinron*, or the study of Japa-neseness, sponsored by one of the leading newspapers in Japan. The intense self-absorption evident in this topic has been publicly evident among Japanese pundits for the past fifty years, and, the newspaper felt, it was time to ring some new changes on the old theme, especially as the outside world seemed to be insisting on "cosmopolitanizing" Japan. Japanese scholars and three or four foreigners were invited to reflect on what it means to be Japanese. We came up with another layer of rhetoric, to wit, the paradoxical statement that the *shinnihonjinron*, or "new Japaneseness," would have to be an *international* identity, rid of the uniqueness and exceptionalism characterizing most previous discussions of Japan and the Japanese. The usual book emerged, and, as usual, the topic submerged yet again. Nonetheless, publicly and privately, many Japanese invoke the new buzzword, *kokusaika*, or "internationalization," as the concept key to Japan's future and as the heart of what they'd like to embody themselves. Why is there such anxiety over Japan's place in the world, precisely at the time when Japan enjoys both domestic prosperity and the greatest success in the international marketplace? Full-scale involvement and success in the world economy does not seem at the moment in any obvious way to threaten Japan's internal cohesion or even its repeatedly flaunted "cultural uniqueness."

It is this last phrase, together with the often invoked "narrow island mentality" that gives some clues about Japanese cultural preferences: the ability to say, "We Japanese are X or believe Y or like Z" with full confidence in an unassailable homogeneity is at the core of Japanese exceptionalism. This may not be the same as nationalistic exclusivity though it does involve a kind of exclusion shown in small and large things: it is very hard for many Japanese to believe that a foreigner can understand or like Japanese things. People often ask me, "Do you really like raw fish?" and when I say I do, they push harder as if to say, surely we can find something she doesn't like — dancing shrimp (alive and wiggling), sea urchin sushi (my favorite kind). I hate to disappoint, and so sometimes I say that it was hard to get to like *natto*, or fermented pickled sticky soybeans.

And it is also expected that all Japanese like such things, that there are no significant differences among people who are Japanese. This minimizing of differences, this homogeneity, is an important construct in Japanese identity, in service to the creation of community. It is a cultural choice: the Japanese value commonality and community, while we Americans have chosen to stress diversity. We both have both, of course, and we Americans have our own insularities. (As a Japanese commentator has asked, "If a person who speaks two languages is bilingual, what do you call a person who speaks only one language?" The answer is, "American.") We continue to feel that anyone with a choice would want to be American, to speak English. The Japanese, on the other hand, prefer to think that only Japanese can really understand the Japanese language. A Japanese sociolinguist, Takao Suzuki, has been quoted in the Japanese newspaper *Asahi Shimbun* as saying, "When a small child begins to toddle about, we praise him with encouraging words, 'Good boy! You can walk!' But if the child were to suddenly stand up and begin to walk about with confidence, we would look horrified, thinking such precociousness strange and uncanny. This is because a small child is not expected to be able to walk . . . like an adult. Likewise it is because we are convinced that foreigners should not be able to speak impeccable Japanese that we feel uncomfortable when we encounter a foreigner whose Japanese is very good."

The Japanese push exceptionalism to neurophysiological extremes, as in the statements that Japanese cannot eat American beef because they have different kinds of intestines, or that Japanese women cannot take the pill because their reproductive organs are different, or that Japanese cannot learn foreign languages easily because the functions of the hemispheres of the brain are reversed. But most people in Japan ultimately do not want to be excluded, or to exclude themselves from more universal definitions of humanity.

I've used the phrase "the intimate community" because I feel the Japanese community is intimate in structure and culture and in the experience of members. Webster's Third International gives a wide range of meanings for the word *intimate* and two capture the flavor of membership in a Japanese group: (1) marked by a very close physical, mental, or social association; and (2) showing complete intermixture, fusion, and interconnection.

The home, or *uchi*, supplies us with the basic model for intimacy, and the earliest experiences of the Japanese child reflect Japanese versions of these meanings. Children are taught, in infancy, that intimate association with others is both the means and the end of life. The word for intimacy is *shitashimi*, using the same character that is used for "parent." Deep association begins at birth. It has been said that the Japanese mother sees her newborn as independent, having separated from her at birth, and needing to be reunited with her into appropriate dependency, for the sake of nurturance and learning. *Amae*, or dependency, does not have the negative meaning it does in American culture, where it is asso-ciated with immaturity and weakness. By contrast, it has been said that the American mother sees the newborn as born dependent, needing to be trained to become independent of her as quickly as possible. One Japanese term for the closeness of mother and child is *skinship* — a word that sounds like English but for which we have no real equivalent — meaning, roughly, the positive intimacy that comes from constant physical closeness. Mothers carry infants in carriers pressing the child to their backs; they bathe with their children and sleep beside them. Mothers rarely employ babysit-ters and do not feel comfortable with nonfamily caretakers.

The seamless bond between mother and child is the goal of this closeness, and it acts as a symbol for the family as well. There are two words, both water metaphors, used frequently to describe the Japanese intimate community: one is *mizuirazu*, the other *nurumayu*. *Mizuirazu* means, literally, "water cannot enter," and is used to describe the watertight closeness of a Japanese family group whose intimacy doesn't let its secrets out, nor outsiders in. This adds a third, very Japanese meaning to the list: intimacy means exclusivity. *Nurumayu* means tepid bath water, the lukewarm water of an infant's bath, and it is used to imply the skin-to-skin shar-ing, the bath water as medium through which the closest contact with another is made, the community of the shared bath. These are very evocative terms to Japanese, who mark intimacy by the literal removal of distance between people.

There is also, ideally, little tension or sense of opposition within the close family. The basic principle of Japanese childrearing is never to go against the child. Externally imposed discipline is rarely used. The assumption is that children are good; all they need is to understand what's wanted and they will do it. The mother first makes sure that the child feels supported and then conveys what's expected. What the mother wants becomes what the child wants. A famous story of the perfect Zen master is used to describe the perfect mother or teacher: the ideal master is someone from whose hand a bird cannot take off, because there is perfect yielding non-resistance in the hand, and thus nothing to take off from, no pur-chase for resistance and flight.

It takes time to achieve this goal; everything, even the reason why you should finish your vegetables, is part of a positive relationship, and you never hear "Because I say so." Rather, it is something like, "Let me tell you about the farmer who grew this cabbage . . ." and if that doesn't work, "The cabbage is very sad that you don't like it." Even public tantrums are handled with infinite patience, and mothers take time to let the child accommodate. This produces what American child psychologists would call merging, and we would say that the child has no space for the growth of what we consider a healthy, independent, autonomous ego. But early autonomy per se is not in the cultural lexicon of Japanese childrearing, and separation is not seen as part of growing up.

In school, too, teachers ideally nurture children. Personal autonomy, in the rugged American sense, is not seen as a prerequisite for academic maturity and creativity. Children are taught to be sensitive to others, to work in teams, to feel safe and secure. In my Japanese dictionary, the example sentence given for the word *intimate* is: "It appears that relationships between students and teachers in this school are not sufficiently *intimate.*" Enthusiasm and mutual support are encouraged and cooperation is not a second-class skill on the report card.

Intimacy and dependency are said to be motivating: Japanese workers are said to perform at high levels because of security, whereas we assume that permanent employment would make people lean on their hoes. Sadaharu Oh, the Babe Ruth of Japan, said that it is by basking in the unconditional love of his mother that he was motivated to struggle harder to perfect his batting stance. While there is in Japan a parallel tradition to our school of hard knocks, in which the older generation says that young ones are going to the dogs, and that hardship builds character, there is little feeling that sparing the parental rod spoils the child. Externally imposed discipline is thought to be of little use in any case.

When the young person enters the workplace, he or she finds another intimate group, another environment which inspires a 100 percent commitment, a new *uchi* or home. When you enter as a new recruit you are a *tabula rasa*, and you need to be trained to the intimate relationships of the work team and company. The traditional Japanese household, like the workplace, sees itself as a special, inward-looking place, with its own culture and even secret lore: the *kafuu* or family ways may be symbolized in things like Grandma's hoarded pickle recipe, or "our house's" way of cele-

brating New Year's. The company, like the household, is an intimate community, even those employing thousands of workers. The
intimacies may be more metaphoric than real, but the assump-
tions of harmony and mutuality, of "insiderness" versus "outsider-
ness" in the company slogan and song, resonate with the assump-
tions of the traditional household.

What is this insiderness and what does the community it represents feel like for the individual? First, that the community is
greater than the sum of its parts and that, to achieve it, everyone
needs to contribute actively — beyond grudging cooperation, team-
work is a premise, and sensitivity an art. Taking care of other people is part of everyone's training, and service is not an extra; it
is basic to all work. There is no tipping for any kind of service
in Japan, and it would be insulting to receive compensation for
the human attentiveness and kindness which are part of the job
description.

Further, it is assumed that people are more comfortable if
they live in a predictable environment. This is supported by ad-
herence to social codes, to systems of appropriate language and
behavior. All of these contribute to a person's sense of how he or
she fits into the social world, helping, it is felt, to produce comfort
for everyone. Sensitivity to others, predictability, the observance
of social codes — all ultimately are aimed at harmony.

The most significant relationships are within a small face-to-
face group where harmony is a concrete reality. Here, in the classroom or work team, the important relationships are forged. But
such work relationships are not goal-oriented in the sense that
American corporate relationships are said to be, and while "networks" and "mentors" are important, they are not created by individuals in service to their own career trajectories. This is far too
self-centered and is seen ultimately as an unrewarding and unhappy strategy. The relationships themselves are the goal, since
it is these that give the workers their identity and these must be
constant, reliable, unconditional — just as is the relationship of
mother and child. Employees feel part of a team more than we
can imagine, we who travel through life identified by portable personal attributes, skills, and credentials, able to drop one corporate setting in favor of another, and for whom institutional loyalty is a wimpy phrase.

There are, however, some negative trade-offs in the Japanese model. While secured intimacy ideally at least is said to promote achievement and while one is comfortably rewarded for this productive harmony, there is little flexibility, little freedom to move beyond the group's borders. Any kind of differentness puts a person at risk, and changing jobs in midcareer is still difficult. Working as a consultant with several companies at once is marginalizing. Organizing people across companies in union work, or across universities in cooperative research, is very difficult. Internal merging is much more important than communication beyond the group's borders. This solidarity depends on long-term mutual habituation and intimate, often unspoken, communication. The phrase *nakama ishiki*, or "group consciousness," is often invoked, and it is a concrete and subtle thing, not like the abstract feeling of loyalty and identity stirred by a pledge of allegiance to a flag or the singing of an anthem. What it takes to create this is more than decoding interpersonal signals, and there is no room in the identity agenda for a completely different set of such signals, those demanded by internationalization.

I conducted a study of Japanese who found themselves in the dilemma of juggling the demands of the intimate domestic workplace and those of international business and trade. These people were full-time employees of large companies, banks, and ministries whose work entailed overseas sojourns of up to five years, and who then returned to Japan to the home offices from which they'd left. A common pattern in the Western world today, in Japan it has created great stress and a popular sense of the "crisis of return" in television specials, soap operas, advice columns in newspapers.

This problem has roots in the demands for intimacy and internal coherence in the Japanese group. The lessons of *inside* and *outside* that are taught in early childhood emphasize the idea that outside is not as acceptable as inside. The central image of insiderhood is that of the home, once again the *uchi*. Children are taught, as we noted earlier, that their own family is special. Nonintimate friends are rarely entertained at home; casual callers are restricted to the *genkan* (entrance hall), where the shoes of those who do enter are left. The *genkan* keeps the house literally clean but also figuratively guards the purity of the inside from the pollution of the outside. And children are taught to avoid the edges of *tatami* (floor matting) and not to step on the wooden beams that mark doorways.

This domestic symbolism adds force to the boundaries confronted later in life. But beyond symbolic ritual is a group's fundamental concern with interpersonal relations, and more important than the symbolic impact of departure is the lesson that members must be predictably and constantly attentive to relations with others. You must be there.

In a traditional rural village one can clearly see the norms of Japanese group membership that lead to the exclusion or stigmatization of those who ignore the necessary face-to-face relationships and of those who cross prohibited boundaries. The small, fixed community of an agricultural village was socially homogeneous, and its cohesion was based on tasks, like the irrigation of paddies, demanding the cooperation of all households. Anything that threatened the relationships integrating a hamlet was a clear violation of group norms and in extreme cases was punished by ostracism. If, for instance, a person passed over the hamlet committee and took grievances to outside legal or political institutions, the group boundaries would have been crossed and its internal problems exposed to the outside world. This was regarded as a breakdown of village cohesion. Typical punishment was to make the offender a hamlet messenger — a go-between role shunned by others.

So an executive returning from overseas today is in many ways similarly blighted. He (these are primarily men) faces a fragile situation at his office, where the requirement of face-to-face relationships has been violated by his absence, and he must deal with a corporate priority of domestic over international work. He may also be watched carefully for signs that he has become a *kokusai-jin*, an "international person." Those who try the hardest to be accepted back wear short, conservative haircuts, dark suits, white shirts, and polished black shoes and deliberately avoid using English words, even those in ordinary business usage in Japan. And still they feel at risk.

While such symbols of cultural conformity help a Japanese group cohere, it would be a mistake to think that the right haircut will do the trick. Cultural traits do not have the same power to cohere in every society. While the French take great pride in their language, food, and art as denominators of cultural identity and may defend this identity with "purify the language" campaigns and gustatorial chauvinism, the Japanese freely indulge in hamburgers and lace their language with words derived from Portuguese, French, German, and English, making it a living record of waves of cultural contact. A Japanese who has never sojourned abroad may grow his hair long or develop a taste for Indian food or dot his speech with English words without arousing suspicion. But returnees who do these things are marked as different because in *them* these things symbolize their physical and temporal absence from the group. For it is social rather than cultural identity that is most important. Active involvement is key. There is no acceptable substitute for being there.

Children returning from overseas with their parents also have problems, and these have even greater visibility in education-conscious Japan. Increasing numbers of children whose background and promise would otherwise place them in line for prestigious academic credentials and work are being locked out. In the press, returnee children are called wounded, victims, pitiful children. The children are said to have had a significantly different experience overseas, one which is supposed to make it difficult for them to work harmoniously with children who have not been abroad, because they have allegedly acquired un-Japanese characteristics. At the same time, in the critical race for academic credentials, these children are said to be handicapped. They have not had as much Japanese language, Japanese-style math, or social studies, nor have they been trained in the special kind of exam taking they will have to undergo.

And so institutions have been created to help them catch up. Both overseas and in Japan, special schools for these children have been established. About 125 schools and classes in Japan are specifically for returnee readjustment, some paid for out of public funds for handicapped children, in which children attempt to catch up to their age level in behavior and cognitive skills before entering an ordinary school.

These latter schools are intended to be temporary remedial way stations, but attendance at these classes often is itself enough to mark children strongly as *internationals*. The stigma of the overseas experience, in fact, is not removed by these schools but in many cases heightened.

Knowledge of small details of classroom custom is part of the reeducation of the child, and readjustment schools emphasize "culture relearning." Teachers and parents call the process *gaikoku nagashi* (peeling off foreignness) and *somenaoshi* (re-dyeing). Teachers say the child must forget foreign experiences as quickly as possible, that there is no room in the head of the child for more than one language. The smallest sign of different behavior in classroom or playground, such as that of a child who in a September heat wave did not wear the standard undershirt, is seen as an indication of contamination by the overseas experience. The mother of a boy who demanded that his lunch include a peanut butter sandwich instead of the usual rice and pickled vegetable was gently chided by the teacher who told her that she should hasten her child's readjustment to Japan, make him more comfortable, by making him a proper lunch. A child who doesn't know the early morning exercise routine is teased by classmates and suffers greatly, even if he'd been on the first string of his school's team in baseball in the United States. All aberrant behavior is attributed to the overseas experience.

We may speculate that the ideal of homogeneity in Japan is not only threatened by international contact but promoted by the process of stigmatization attached to that contact. The returnee symbolizes transgression and thereby represents a sort of photographic negative of the Japanese ideal. These people are useful to society as markers of the boundary between the acceptable and the inappropriate. The damaged identity of the returnee who has gone beyond the pale outweighs the attractive aspects of international work. Never mind that the work such people have done, and do, is critically important to the continuing prosperity of Japan, even to the maintenance of the coherent domestic style which is so threatened by an international's supposedly contaminated work habits.

It is too abstract and almost meaningless to say that Japan as a nation is the intimate family writ large, a kind of *macro-uchi*, and that this accounts for the difficulties of international communication and negotiation. It is also not enough to say, as some Japanese themselves say, that the period of almost three hundred

years of seclusion which ended in 1868 produced such cultural cohesion and self-sufficient insularity that it is hard still to overcome
its effects. Nor, finally, is Japanese resistance to thoroughgoing internationalization a product of economic and policy structures and
procedures programmed to preserve the complex domestic inter-
relationships between business and government.

It may, however, be a mixture of all these and is ultimately
a much more difficult and interesting problem than any of these.
Akio Morita and Shintaro Ishihara have recently discussed it in
their book *The Japan That Can Say No*. This book, in bootlegged
translation, circulates in photocopy in the United States, but it
was intended as part of an internal Japanese discussion. Its authors now claim it was not to be a document officially entered
into the United States–Japan dialogue. That claim itself is a piece
of the very problem we are discussing. A best-selling book in Japan
was not expected to be read by outsiders? The implication is that
we are prying into family secrets; that, written in Japanese, it was
safe from us. The book does read like an internal dialogue, with
occasionally a rather shrill piece of rhetoric, perhaps in response
to the recent scandals weakening the ruling LDP and to recent
consumer outcries at high prices of land, housing, and consumer
goods and the imposition of a sales tax. What the authors advo-
cate now is for Japan to speak out, and up, and to communicate
directly, to be straightforward and critical with Americans. Japanese, they claim, need an "international" style to avoid being taken
advantage of — to avoid losing their identity. The threat of this loss
is the core of such recent *nihonjinron* statements and explains both
the rhetoric and the strange privacy in these utterances.

American debates have contributed to *nihonjinron* self-
absorption: we have accused Japan of not playing by international
rules for historical, structural, cultural, or other special reasons;
and some even claim that Japan needs special treatment if it is
not to destroy the international economic order. These arguments
stem from basic *nihonjinron*. And, in response, Ishihara claims that
American reaction to Japan is racist, that we would not behave
the same way with European trading partners.

Racism has been in evidence within Japan as well, however,
another aspect of the insularity of this particular intimate community. Former Prime Minister Nakasone is infamous in the United

States for his remark that low American educational levels are a result of the large numbers of blacks and Hispanics in the population, and it was recently reported that the mayor of Kawaguchi stated that Japanese in his town have trouble at night seeing the many dark-skinned Pakistanis who now work there. Citing three hundred years of seclusion and more racial homogeneity than other modern societies exhibit cannot wash out those spots. It's not enough to say that the Japanese are not yet diplomatically savvy, are not yet sensitive to other cultures and ideologies.

Change must come. Those Pakistanis in Kawaguchi represent only a small percentage of those who are breaking through the homogeneity myth in Japan, and already it is more than international diplomacy that will demand openness and sensitivity. Japan's labor force needs workers for less skilled, lower paid work for which young Japanese are overqualified, or in any event won't take; and many have come from southeastern and southern Asia already — up to 400,000, most as illegal immigrants on faked student visas. The Japanese need them but persist in what can only be called racial prejudice. The National Police Agency admitted to circulating a memo to police stations saying that Pakistanis have "a unique body odor, carry diseases, and lie in the name of Allah." This was retracted and there was an official apology. But it wasn't so long ago that Americans were called *batakusai* (butter-smelling) and Koreans, "garlic-smelling." And a recent Harris poll in Japan showed that 42 percent believe that America's economic problems are caused by "too many different minorities." There will soon be a critical mass of "different" people in Japan, and Japanese will have to come to terms with diversity.

The British have a way of discussing heterogeneity to which they refer as "racialism" as opposed to racism, and it has been suggested that we look at Japanese statements as the former, connoting only that a difference is noted, rather than the latter, which implies that some action or program is adopted on the basis of differentness. However, if people noted as "different" suffer in any way by being so noted — for example, being denied citizenship, having to be regularly fingerprinted, being locked out of opportunities for certain kinds of employment, or, as in the case of several American baseball players in Japan, being prevented from going to bat lest they top a Japanese top hitter's record—then we must question the application of the British distinction to Japan.

On the other hand, in one of the most traditional of Japanese pastimes, sumo wrestling, most Japanese are unequivocally delighted with their new American champion, the 490-pound Konishiki. (One Japanese novelist, however, said that if he reached the top rank, all tournaments should be called off, in shame that an American beat out the Japanese. It hit too close to home for him.)

For the individual, the intimate community of family and small group provides elements that are undeniably Good Things, things we would want too. Support, continuity, security are rewards everyone can grasp, not conditional on personal achievement or credentials to the degree that worth and reward are measured in the West. There is social and personal value attached to cooperation, service, and sharing as qualities potential and credited in everyone.

There is cost, however. There is worse than risk attached to voluntary or involuntary differentness, to being off-course or off-schedule, to attempting anything not on track, especially as an individual. There are, of course, plenty of examples of nonmainstream groups that have changed Japan, that have resisted and won: consumer movement groups, groups supporting minority education programs, antipollution campaigns, political and religious groups making themselves heard. Even some individuals, women and men, speaking out have made a difference. Japan is *not* a stagnant society, and it is not an ideological dictatorship: what we would call constraints on individual freedoms are subtle, not top-down and not formal. Our own emphasis on freedom under law, on contractual relationships, and on the individual as the empowered unit in society represents a very different model and of course not a uniformly experienced reality. It may be informative and illuminating to look at the United States as a most exotic case: we are not like the rest of the world. As one writer has said, we have prescribed individualism to a degree often isolating, dislocating, and uncomfortable for individuals and families and ultimately negating the idea of society itself. Our interest in promoting diversity too is often at odds with our own intimate communities' needs for identity and commonality. Rather than to see Japan as a hermetically sealed society powered by structured conformist agenda, a special case enemy to the free market, it may be more helpful to see Japan as unevenly developed — where what I call the intimate communities that typified most societies before modernization have weight and worth, but where a flexible and internationally sensitive national framework has not completely emerged. If the Japanese can gain the latter without losing the support and solace of the former, we all may have much to learn.

6

Ritual and the Symbolic Geography of Community

KATHERINE PLATT

SITTING IN A CAFE IN TUNIS or at the shrine of Sidi Mansour in the city of Sfax or at the village well in Ouled Bou Ali on the Kerkennah Islands, if you were to ask someone, "Who are you?" the first response would not be, "My name is Salah" or "I am the son of Habib" or "I am a teacher" or "I am a Muslim" or "I am a Tunisian." The first response would most likely be, "I am from such and such a place." The answer refers to a specific location, a landscape, a settlement, an identifiable place to which people tie their identities. This anchor of identity remarkably is often a place away from which the respondent's family had migrated a generation or even two back.

During the course of nearly two years' anthropological fieldwork on the Kerkennah Islands of Tunisia and in the mainland cities of Sfax and Tunis, I was struck by the consistently geographical response to the question, "Who are you?" I was even more struck during the two summers I was there to watch the Kerkennah population of 15,000 swell to 50,000 as these desert islands became overrun with labor migrants, returning to their place of origin for the wedding season and for the celebration of numerous other life cycle and Islamic rituals.

I was captivated by the following questions: What is the meaning of this place for all these people? How does this meaning persist over these periods of absence, sometimes as long as someone's working life? Some are over great distances, as far away as Tunis, Marseilles, Paris, Frankfurt, Montreal. Is the meaning of place different for those who stay and for those who leave? How do these differences of meaning get communicated and negotiated when the migrating and home populations congregate? How is this meaning of place symbolized by those who leave? How is it commemorated, preserved, reconstituted, or ritualized in the distant places of migration? How is the meaning of place controlled and regulated by those who stay, the guardians of place?

All of these questions point to the underlying problem of the construction and maintenance of social identity. A community once unified by common residence in a geographical location is dispersed by the centrifuge of labor migration. Community still exists, but it is no longer defined by residence. And place is no longer just a location, a common dwelling; place becomes both a portable and necessary symbol of identity for those who leave and a valuable form of symbolic capital for those who stay.

For the community, no longer *in* a common place, being *of* a common place takes on a new meaning.[1] There is a particular emotional charge to this because the claim to being *of* a common place is not automatically valid. The claim must be legitimated by those who control the symbolic capital of place — in other words, those who are both *in* and *of* the place of origin. These claims and evaluations are intensely negotiated, although somewhat indirectly, in the celebrations of both life cycle rituals and annual Islamic holiday rituals which swell the island population like a pot of steamed couscous.

This paper develops a definition of community that does not make a simple social-spatial association but which, at the same time, recognizes and integrates the different symbolic-spatial associations with place of origin. It will be a definition that also recognizes and integrates the different demands that various components of the community make upon their common identity.

My basic argument is this: one's identity as a man, a woman, and a Muslim of good reputation and right practice is established and renewed through a series of life cycle rituals and annual Islamic holidays. In order to be effective, these rituals must take place in a social field void of anonymity and which is a complete moral universe.[2] This means that all moral categories including the poor and the dead are present. In terms of both status enhancement and moral authority, the rituals must take place in a context of shared meanings, shared information, and shared standards of evaluation. The place of origin reliably provides such a context for those both *in* and *of* the place of origin. As such, the place, itself, becomes a powerful symbol of orthopraxy, especially for those who live away.

Community involves the recognition and maintenance of a common system of mutual evaluation. This does not mean, of course, that people do not submit themselves to multiple systems of evaluation and social control. They do. But community can be partially defined in terms of the system of evaluation that they all share at least temporarily. Rituals provide both the standard and the opportunity for such an evaluation. This standard depends on a common store of information about the behavior, prospects, failures, and reputations of participating individuals. Such information is necessarily transmitted orally; it is planted in the soil of social memory and irrigated by the regular rotations of the gossip mill. Such an oral tradition, of course, requires regular face-to-face relations which the summer wedding season provides in the most graphic sense.

This definition of community is dynamic in the sense that it recognizes varying degrees of attachment and attraction to the place of origin. There are many of these. On the continuum of commitment, by which people identify themselves as members of the community, the minimum yet sufficient criterion is mutual participation in life cycle and annual Islamic rituals.[3] This involves people in a vast network of delayed reciprocity, a system of mutual social and moral evaluation, and a commitment to at least one intersecting set of norms, all of which are symbolized by the place of origin.

But why is it that being *of* a place is so important to labor migrants making their way in urban industrial capitalism? What do they have to gain from a connection to a world of peasant subsistence? From a psychological point of view, it's easy to imagine that identification with place of origin is an important anchor in an insecure and unfamiliar world. But identity with place of origin is not just of compensatory, therapeutic value. Paradoxically, while it grounds people to their symbolic roots, it also lubricates their mobility into this unfamiliar world. As in many other places in North Africa and the Middle East, economic and political networks in Tunisia, even in the modern sector, are largely organized on the basis of local ties. Access to various economic specialties and political opportunities are afforded by a validated claim to membership in the home community. For example, the trade union movement in Tunisia is dominated by Kerkennis because the founder, Farhat Hached, who was martyred in the struggle for independence, was a local boy. Railroad and customs jobs as well as the National Fisheries Office are also Kerkennah specialties. Similarly, the newspaper industry is dominated by people from the southern Tunisian town of Chenini,[4] and the grocery trade is dominated by migrants from Djerba. These closed rivers of local identity run through the national economic and political arena.

This same dynamic pertains in a more diffuse way in international migration. It is estimated that between 13 and 20 percent of Tunisia's active labor force is in international migration. Ninety percent of these migrants work in France, largely in the south, as industrial and agricultural laborers. In international migration, it is unlikely that a local Tunisian group will wield any special political weight, but the residential and occupational concentration of individuals from very specific localities is well documented.[5]

Clearly, it does not make sense to talk about labor migration as if it were a single or simple phenomenon. Rural urban migration taking place within the nation-state is ever on the increase. Fifty percent of the Tunisian population of 7 million now lives in urban areas as opposed to 25 percent in 1931. Twenty percent of the total population lives in Tunis and 9 percent in Sfax. These cities together receive 75 percent of all Kerkenni migrants. Tunis is growing at 5 percent a year compared to a national growth rate of 2.5 percent and a rural growth rate of 1 percent.[6] Statistically, rural-urban migration in Tunisia is a one-way street. In actuality, this one-way street has a number of little countercurrents running through it, and these countercurrents have a lot of significance for the topic at hand, the nonspatial definition of a *local* community.

Most rural-urban movement is part of a phenomenon called chain migration in which, over a period of time, successful migrants from a particular place pull other individuals to whom they are historically linked into their new location and occupation. This is usually accompanied by another phenomenon called replacement migration in which migrants from a particular location re-place each other in the urban slots that their group has been able to carve out and protect. So even while the numerical trend is toward permanent migration to urban areas, a significant portion of this group circulates back to the home place for long periods of time. In other words, the very personnel who fill the category of migrant, at some other time in their life cycles might fill the category of homebound. This dynamic is important in the maintenance of a local identity.

In international migration, because most migrants are employed in insecure manual jobs and because of the constraints of work permits and other political and cultural factors, eventual return migration is the norm.[7] People usually go with the expectation that they will return for good, if only in retirement. This expectation is accompanied over the long term by certain preparations for the eventual return, including seasonal visits, building of holiday or retirement villas, sending of remittances and other material goods, as well as subsidizing expensive rituals in the place of origin.

In my view, it makes very little sense to try to understand labor migration in North Africa and the Middle East in terms of the motivations and opportunities of autonomous individuals. Demographic studies based on head counts encourage us to do this. There are few attempts to integrate rigorous statistical materials with qualitative models that pay attention to individual migration as part of a wider family survival strategy or the nonmaterial centripetal force of the place of origin. It is to these two issues that I now turn my attention.

The local Kerkennah economy is a subsistence economy based on small-scale fishing and agriculture subject to a quite neat sexual division of labor between these two activities. The work of James Scott has been very helpful to me in gaining an understanding of what a subsistence economy means in terms of community and local identity. In his book about Southeast Asian peasant rebellions called *The Moral Economy of the Peasant*, Scott gives an extraordinarily lucid account of what subsistence means to peasants in terms of their perception of the choices available to them. Scott's main point is that what he calls the "subsistence ethic" is risk-averse and geared to minimizing the possibility of a major loss rather than maximizing the possibility of a major gain. It is a "safety-first" economic outlook which is reinforced by many of the social arrangements that characterize a traditional village culture. He argues that the patterns of reciprocity, forced generosity, communal land, and work sharing, and even systems of gossip and envy, are redistributive mechanisms. These promote the achievement of a subsistence standard of living for all the members of the community, the right to which is seen as a basic principle of social justice. These features give traditional peasant culture the appearance of being radically and morally egalitarian when, in fact, these defenses against inequality and autonomy are really practical devices for insuring a minimum standard of living.

Discussing the communitarian tradition and village morality in Southeast Asia, Scott notes:

> Village redistribution worked unevenly and, even at its best, produced no egalitarian utopia. We may suppose that there was always some tension in the village between the better-off who hoped to minimize their obligations and the poor who had the most to gain from communal social guarantees. The poor, for their part, got "a place," not an equal income, and must have suffered a loss of status as a result of their permanent dependence. Nevertheless, this pattern did represent the minimal moral requirements of village mutuality. It worked through the support or acquiescence of most villagers and, above all, in normal times it assured the "survival of the weakest." What moral solidarity the village possessed *as a village* was in fact based ultimately on its capacity to protect and feed its inhabitants. So long as village membership was valuable in a pinch, the "little tradition" of village norms and customs would command a broad acceptance.[8]

The Kerkennah moral economy fits Scott's model of the subsistence ethic quite closely. I would argue that this principle of mutuality which provides for "the survival of the weakest" can equally well be applied to the community in its broadest definition, that is, the community *of* as well as *in* Kerkennah.

One of the principles of the subsistence ethic is to distribute risk as a way of stabilizing the system, hence the lack of specialization in peasant economies. Kerkennis plant small amounts of a number of different crops; they use a variety of fishing traps and techniques; they own small stakes in several communally held resources such as olive and palm groves and fresh water cisterns. In the same subsistence spirit, labor migration is yet another way for peasant families to distribute their risks. The ideal configuration is for one or more adult sons to stay on the islands to pursue subsistence activities and maintain the family property and for one or more sons to be sent to the mainland to pursue a profession or trade, or more likely just to work for a wage. This insures the flow of some cash through remittances into the family budget and the safety net of several functioning traditional enterprises back on the islands should things not go well. And they often do not. Tunisian unemployment figures hover around 25 percent, and I have already mentioned the special insecurities of working in a foreign economy.

Seen from this perspective, labor migration is less a move toward economic modernization and integration into the national economy than a conservative stability-seeking strategy entirely consistent with the subsistence ethic. This is only evident, however, if one takes into account the degree to which families with adult sons operate as risk-reducing collective units in which, paradoxically, one of the strategies is to send sons out as risk-taking labor migrants.

Labor migration is a conservative move in another way. Cash remittances are almost never invested in local capital enterprises. They are used instead for ordinary consumption needs, to enhance the lifestyle of the family with home improvements and appliances, and to finance rituals.[9] Consequently, the gains from participation in the modern economy serve to stabilize and subsidize the traditional economy rather than transforming it in such a way that migration for cash employment might be unnecessary.

Risk reduction is one of the features of the subsistence ethic. Redistribution of resources to reduce material inequality is another feature. All of the uses to which remittances are put serve to reduce inequality between the migrant and the home community, between branches of extended families, and between adult brothers. Capital investment would widen these gaps.

Risk spreading, familism as economic strategy, redistribution rather than investment of resources, and labor migration as a subsidy for the local subsistence economy — all are ways that the community in its wider sense submits itself to a common standard of moral and social evaluation. Certainly, as Scott says, some of the better-off members try to escape the demands of the subsistence ethic by minimizing their identification with Kerkennah. Many labor migrants participate in more than one system of social evaluation, and many migrants have no active economic interest in the islands. What remains, however, at the minimal end of the continuum of commitment and involvement is a large population of migrants who feel it necessary and desirable to mark the most important transitions in their life cycles and the most important moments in the religious year with extensive, expensive, and — dare I say — exhausting celebrations on Kerkennah, the place of origin.

Because of this, of all the redistributive mechanisms, investment and participation in the life cycle and Islamic rituals are the most comprehensive. In the summer the population triples as permanent and temporary migrants, people *of* Kerkennah, come back to attend engagements, weddings, circumcision ceremonies, celebratory visits to local saints' shrines, and Islamic feasts. These latter lunar holidays, of course, occur earlier every year, but the years I was on Kerkennah (1977–78), the two major Islamic feasts occurred during the summer wedding season, which added to the intensity of the atmosphere.

There is no single event in Kerkenni life that provides more excitement, entertainment, and intrigue, or involves so many people and so much cost as the marriage ritual. Kerkennah endogamy is still a strong pattern even among long-term labor migrants. Even if the intended bride and groom both live in Tunis, the many ritual components of the wedding process — from engagement through the final "thanking" of the bride's father seven days after the actual wedding — take place on the island. These events are often spread over a five-year period as the necessary resources are accumulated and circulated. At minimum, there are fourteen separate prescribed public events during all of the phases of the process. The *public* character can expand to include the entire village of origin and all those who identify themselves as *of* that village, or contract to the immediate families involved, depending on the particular event. At any rate, a successfully completed wedding will have occasioned many, many reunions of the migrating and home components of the community. The sheer circulation of personnel is staggering.

Equally remarkable is the circulation of money, gifts, jewelry, clothing, and furniture. In this minimum structure of fourteen events, I recorded thirty-seven separate obligatory exchanges between different involved parties, ranging from the bride and the groom and their families, the musicians, the midwife, the notary, and the guests, to the camel who finally carries the bride to her groom's family home. These exchanges are in addition to the actual bridewealth and trousseau that the groom and bride provide and the contributions of labor and services — cleaning, cooking, transporting, and lending of space and household goods — that local residents provide.

As these people and goods circulate, a tremendous amount of information is being generated. There is explicit information circulating about courtships, marriage negotiations, business deals, crop failures, thefts, adulteries, pilgrimages, deaths, and so on. This explicit level of discourse takes place in the face-to-face encounters of the many wedding events. Then there is an implicit dance of signals about closeness, distance, forgiveness, alliance, filial devotion, sibling solidarity, and so on which takes place within the code of generosity and participation. This latter category of information in particular is minutely recorded in the social memory of the community.

The depth, breadth, and precision of this memory bank is an important form of insurance. Because of it, those distant cousins who contribute money for the wedding jewelry, lend their car, travel to the islands from France three summers in a row, and dance until dawn on the wedding night, can count on the same show of support plus interest when their own time comes.

These people go away confident that these debts and the statement they make about the social and moral character of the creditor have been securely registered. As such, the islands are the place where people are most deeply *known*, and the site of this shared social memory becomes a symbol of this knowledge and hence a symbol of the labor migrant's self-esteem.

Annual Islamic rituals do not entail such a vast redistribution of property but they do entail much movement of personnel, in circuits of reciprocal visiting and hospitality. In addition to

promenading, sharing of food, and formal visiting, other important elements of the major feasts are Qur'an readings over the graves
of deceased family members and the giving of alms to the poor.
These are pan-Islamic rituals which celebrate the Dar el Islam,
but they are also insular rituals which celebrate the community
as *communitas* by diminishing the distinguishing barriers between
the different components of the population.[10] The sharing of special and symbolic foods is the most elemental form of cohesion,
the holiday promenades are a relaxation of the boundaries of the
female domestic domain, the celebrations of kin entice the mainland Kerkennis back and disguise their distinguishing affluence,
the alms and offerings to the poor pull them closer and diminish
their distinguishing poverty, and the graveyard readings beckon
back the community that has died.

    These last two things are particularly important because the
moral universe upon which the efficacy of these rituals depends
would not be complete without these moral categories, the poor
and the dead, being present.[11] These two essential categories are
necessarily connected with the place of origin. If at all possible,
given the need to bury someone within twenty-four hours, people
are buried in the graveyard of their ancestral village. There are
five religious occasions during the year that call for a Qur'an reading over the graves of the deceased. The giving of alms is one of
the pillars of Islam. The moral category of the poor is a problematic one for labor migrants, especially for those who go abroad.
Although it requires a certain amount of economic mobility to be
able to go abroad to work, *in the migrant situation* labor migrants
are usually at the bottom of the heap. In that context, relatively
speaking, *they* are poor, although they do not see themselves that
way. On Kerkennah, they decidedly are *not* poor, and they know
very well who is. Traditionally, the poor, widowed, and handicapped who live nearby become attached in a semipermanent way
to particular extended families. Year after year on the Feast of the
Sacrifice each family knows to whom it will give the prized right
shoulder of the lamb and other alms. The essential categories of
the moral universe in the place of origin are unambiguous and
clearly defined. The place of origin is a complete moral universe.

    Kerkennis feel that simply being a Kerkenni gives them a head
start on being a good Muslim, that their social and physical en-

vironment aids them in following the straight path (*el mustagim*). They also feel that other environments make it difficult for people to be good Muslims. Kerkennis say that the simplicity and hardiness of their diet, fish and grain which they catch and produce themselves, makes them stronger than other people and more able to fast during Ramadan and still work hard, which is what God wants. They say they are closer to God because everything they require comes directly from the sky, the sea, or the earth. They also say that the peaceful conditions make it possible for them to contemplate the Qur'an and to give proper attention to their prayers. The lack of anonymity is given as the reason that there are no beggars on Kerkennah.

In addition to being better able to do what is religiously required, they see themselves as less vulnerable to those things which are forbidden. These kinds of statements are given by Kerkennis of both sexes and of varying ages as well as by mainland Kerkennis.

It is not unusual for a community to think that its religious practices are correct and orthodox or more so than some other place. What is interesting in the case of Kerkennah is the way in which they see their setting, the locality itself, as providing the *means* to correct practice. There is a sense of privileged access to big-tradition pan-Islamic orthodoxy through their connection with this specific place.[12] This is not the same as privileged access to God through the intercession of saints, even when the saint has sanctified a particular location. Kerkennis do see their islands, not as a sacred place, but rather as an austere guide to a proper Islamic life, similar to the role of the Qur'an.

When a man goes out on Kerkennah, he is a public figure. When he goes out in Tunis or Marseilles, he is a stranger. Association with the place of origin, as the repository of personal honor and the symbol of right practice, is the antidote to this most painful feature of urban industrial life: anonymity.

NOTES

1. David Stephenson, "Migration and Community," in *Change in Tunisia*, ed. Russell Stone and John Simmons (Albany: State University of New York Press, 1976). This article develops the definition of a com-

munity that shares a system of social organization but is located in more than one place.

2. I am using the idea of the moral community as it was developed by Pnina Werbner in "Sealing the Koran: Offering and Sacrifice among Pakistani Labour Migrants," *Cultural Dynamics* 1 (1988): 77–93.

3. I owe the idea of a "continuum of commitment" to Graeme J. Hugo, "Circulation in West Java, Indonesia," in *Circulation in the Third World*, ed. R. M. Prothero and Murray Chapman (London: Routledge & Kegan Paul, 1985), pp. 75–99.

4. Stephenson, "Migration and Community."

5. Laurence Michelak, "The Impact of Continuing and Return Migration from Tunisia: Case Studies from the Tunisian Northwest" (Paper presented at the Twenty-second Annual Meeting of the Middle East Studies Association, Beverly Hills, California, November 2–5, 1988), p. 3.

6. Kenneth Perkins, *Tunisia: Crossroads of the Islamic and European Worlds* (Boulder, Colo.: Westview Press, 1986), p. 6.

7. Michelak, "The Impact of Continuing," p. 3.

8. James Scott, *The Moral Economy of the Peasant* (New Haven, Conn.: Yale University Press, 1976), pp. 43–44.

9. See also A. Najib, *Migration of Labour and the Transformation of the Economy of the Wedinoon Region of Morocco* (Uppsala: Uppsala University Press, n.d.).

10. See Victor Turner, *The Ritual Process* (Chicago: Aldine Press, 1969).

11. See Werbner, "Sealing the Koran."

12. See McKim Marriott, "Little Communities in an Indigenous Civilization," *American Anthropologist* 57, no. 3, Memoir 83 (1955) for a rich account of the dynamism between the parochial and the universal in an Indian village culture.

7

Chinese Culture and
the Concept of Community

BENJAMIN SCHWARTZ

THE WORD *COMMUNITY* has loomed large in the intellectual discourse of the modern West ever since the nineteenth century. At times the word is used very loosely and broadly as a synonym for the word *society*, or as a way of referring to all the social dimensions of human life. At other times it is used very specifically and precisely to refer to the concept of community enshrined in Ferdinand Tönnies's distinction between "community" (*Gemeinschaft*) and "society" (*Gesellschaft*).

Whether used broadly or narrowly, however, it is often closely coupled with its binary opposite, *the individual* or *individualism*. In countless textbooks we find the cliche that while traditional societies are marked by the dominance of the community, modern society is marked by the dominance of the individual. Similarly, non-Western societies which remain traditional are communitarian while modern Western society is individualistic. For those who long for a simple dyadic formula to sum up the differences between Chinese and Western culture, this formula immediately springs to mind.

All of these terms relate to the social dimension of human life. Even *individualism* is, after all, a social doctrine. All of these categories relate to levels and types of human relationships whether they refer to cultural systems, social systems, economic systems, or various types of group entities. I shall, with fear and trembling, attempt to say something about the nature of that vast area we refer to as religion without, of course, attempting to define it. Yet in the modern world when one is asked to relate religion or philosophy or ethics or literature to some aspect of society, there is quite often the strong presumption that one is being asked to explain how these traits of the spirit have been produced by the social formation, or how they are "functional" to the social formation, just as the psychologist will insist that they are caused by or are functional to human psychological structures. Thus in many of the textbooks I have mentioned, a profound link is discerned between religion and community. Since both religion and community belong to "traditional society," there is a presumption of an organic link between the two. Thus in Durkheim religion tends to be a projection of those "representative ideas" which maintain the solidarity of the community. Modern individualism, on the other hand, marks a break, for good or ill, with both community and religion and represents the secularization of humankind. In this view the very existence or nonexistence of religion is a by-product of social formations.

One might ask why this kind of social explanation enjoys the persuasive power which it seems to enjoy in modern society. What accounts for the enormous ontic weight which we assign to social formations and forces? I suggest that it has a good deal to do with the post-Cartesian radical disjunction between the human realm and the cosmic realm. For Descartes the cosmos is wholly assigned to the modern physical sciences and has little to say to human beings in any sphere other than the technical and the contemplation of mathematical truth. While a human being is tied to nature by his or her body, which is one mechanism among others, the center of the human's being as human is his or her own individual subjectivity. The locus of this anthropocentrism is the individual human subject.

It does not take long, however, for others such as Giambattista Vico to point out that to locate the essence of the human wholly in the individual human subject is to provide a radically defective account of the human realm. It is to ignore completely the plural, social aspect of human life which expresses itself through all the realities which we now call social, cultural, economic, historic, and so forth. The vast bulk of humanity does not embody the transcendent rationality which Descartes ascribes to himself. On the contrary, it is these social realities which shape and determine the human subject rather than the reverse. But this outlook is just as anthropocentric as the Cartesian. These social entities and social systems also lack a source in the cosmic order. The disjuncture between humanity and the universe remains, but now the main causes for human behavior and human beliefs must be sought within these supraindividual entities and processes.[1] As Marx states in his *Theses on Feuerbach*, the "essence" of the human is not to be sought in the "isolated individual" but in the "ensemble of social relations."[2]

One is immediately struck by the enormous ontic weight which is assigned to these categories. They refer to entities which become highly demarcated, and they are all endowed with enormous dynamic causal power. When Marx uses the term "essence of man," this includes causative power.[3] Human consciousness and behavior are determined *either* by the isolated individual *or* by the "ensemble of social relations." Just as in a theological age theological categories became sharply demarcated, reified, and absolutized, in a "social scientific" age the fiercest doctrinal conflicts will arise over the conflicting causal claims of various social "isms" such as individualism, socialism, capitalism, communitarianism, and the like.

I do not mean to imply here that before the modern disjuncture between the cosmic and the human realms there had been no debates concerning problems we now call social, cultural, or economic. I would nevertheless suggest that so long as there existed the belief that the nonhuman cosmos was a source of meaning and values and even of determinative power within the human realm, the categories of the social sciences did not possess the dogmatic determinative weight which they have come to possess in a totally anthropocentric world. The "causes" of human action did not spring entirely from either a totally autonomous individual "imperial subject" or totally autonomous social entities or processes.

Now in dealing with the relationship between religion and community, I shall in the first instance focus my attention on the precise, narrower Tönnies conception of community as *Gemeinschaft*. I shall also refer to Martin Buber, whose concept of community is significantly different from that of Tönnies. I shall concentrate on this concept because somehow it seems to relate to religion in an infinitely more intimate way than does the opposing category of *Gesellschaft*. In fact, Martin Buber calls *Gesellschaft* "collectivism"; and Max Weber speaks of *Gesellschaft* as a vast machine systematically designed to achieve certain individual and collective goals of wealth and power through the application of rational means to the achievement of these rational ends. In Buber's words, in collectivism as opposed to community "the only important thing in groups in the present as in history is what they aim at and what they accomplish,"[4] rather than the sense of social fellowship and warm interrelationship of the "I and Thou" which is not instrumental to some further end but is a consummatory good in itself. Within a community the bonds which unite an *I* and a *Thou* are extended to embrace a *we*.

For Tönnies and Weber, both the contractual relations of individuals in a capitalist economy and the rational organization of a modern bureaucracy are based on a machine-like rationality of ends and means (*Zwecksrationalität*). There is in fact no contradiction between "atomic individualism" and *Gesellschaft*. Whether one is a worker, a business executive, or a bureaucrat totally subjugated to some future collective end, all of these roles are *gesellschaftlich*. What is *religious* about a community is, at least in Buber, the fact that an individual does not achieve personhood by being a self-enclosed "atomic individual" but by being related in the present to the significant Other, whether this other is God or other human beings. The relationship with others is constitutive of the person him- or herself. To Weber, *Gesellschaft* is profoundly irreligious because, whether it is concerned with individual or collective goals, it applies to both the same technological attitudes it applies to the cosmos itself. Nature is treated as an instrument to certain ulterior "rational" ends in the same way as society.

Tönnies regards himself as thoroughly irreligious and emphasizes the "natural" basis of the community as opposed to the artificial nature of *Gesellschaft*. As in Weber, this notion rests on the conscious, deliberate application of rational means to the achievement of rational goals. To someone interested in Chinese thought it is striking that, like Confucius, he finds in the family the first and most concrete paradigm of the community. The family, we are told, is a *Gemeinschaft* because "the natural relationship is by its very essence of earlier origin than its subjects or members."[5] One might say that the natural relationship is based on something like the biological programming of the social animals rather than on any deliberate purpose. The love and mutuality which characterize the family "naturally" arises out of and is functional to these preestablished relations. What is more, Tönnies reminds us of Confucianism to the extent that unlike some forms of nineteenth-century romantic communitarianism, he by no means assumes that community presupposes a total egalitarianism or collapse of all forms and rituals. The ascribed roles of the family presuppose a natural hierarchy, and the authority of the father is almost the prototype of all *Gemeinschaft*-like "natural authority."

To be sure, we shall find that Tönnies's conception of nature, which is based on what he regards as a scientific naturalism, may turn out to be quite different from the "nature" of Confucius. It is also true that Tönnies applies the concept of *Gemeinschaft* to social entities which in Confucius might be problematic or even nonexistent. Presumably a rural village, even though it is not based on kinship, is a *Gemeinschaft* because it is based on "natural conditions" in its relationship to the soil. The bond of soil and field even tends to replace the bond of common ancestry. The ancient city-state, which was based on a need for common defense, was a *Gemeinschaft*. Finally even something as vast as *das Volk*, "the people-nation," because it is bound by the "natural condition" of a common language, can be thought of as nation-community *(Volksgemeinschaft)*. Again, to those who think of community in terms of a visible group in constant face-to-face communion, this may seem to be a strange and even ominous extension of the idea.

There is a distinction between Tönnies's concept of community as a "natural growth" and Buber's conception of community as based on a kind of consummatory "I and Thou" relationship. While Tönnies does in one place speak of friendship as a *Gemeinschaft*-like relationship even though friendship does not arise out of natural relations, he does not seem to have favored deliberate attempts on the part of nineteenth- and twentieth-century idealists to create communities. Buber, who was not so wedded to the notion of community as a natural growth, was, of course, very much interested in the youth movement communities in Weimar Germany as well as in the kibbutzim in Israel. When we contemplate these efforts to create communal life by deliberate decision, we are struck by the fact that the most enduring of such communal experiments have not been based on the idea of the "religion of the community" as such. They have been based, rather, on a commitment to religious ideas which transcend the distinction between individuals and community, as in the case of the Amish, the Shakers, Hutterites, or Orthodox Jews, for whom the community is functional to their religion rather than the reverse. Within such communities an enormous amount of attention is devoted to the moral and religious cultivation of the individuals who make up the community. There is no expectation that merely living within the orbit of the organic entity known as a community will automatically transform the members of the community. Those within our modern secular world who mourn the "loss of community," like the founders of Brook Farm or the youth of the sixties who founded communes, often expected *community* to perform this magical transformation without in the least modifying their personal lifestyles. Conversely, those who remain committed to a rationalist individualism and to *Gesellschaft* as a rational goal-oriented project often deplore talk of community precisely because of its supposed religious overtones. To them religion, like community, suggests the authority of the other imposed on the individual; they ignore all the servitudes imposed by modern *Gesellschaft* of which Weber was so acutely aware. Religion is thus totally identified with the dominance of the individual by society.

All of this, of course, totally overlooks the fact that much of the history of Western religion has been obsessed with the relationship of the individual, rather than of the community, to the divine. Kierkegaard's almost frenzied emphasis on the "single one," and his rejection of human social life as representing an obstacle to the communication between God and human beings, may be an extreme reaction to Hegel's lifelong effort to identify the World Spirit not so much with community as with the entire sociopolitical history of humanity. While both Kierkegaard and Hegel were religious, they were also modern; and their extreme positions on the relationship of religion to the individual and the social may have, after all, reflected the dogmatism of modern social thought. Yet there can be no doubt that the emphasis on the relationship of the individual soul to God has been a central theme of the Judeo-Christian tradition as a whole.

On the other side, it can not be denied that religion has also played an enormous role in the legitimization of many of the most *gesellschaftlich* aspects of our societies. In nineteenth-century Russia, the Slavophiles who claimed to base their views on Russian Orthodox theology drew a sharp distinction between the sacred *sobornost* or communitarianism of the Russian village and the detestable *gesellschaftlichkeit* of the Petrine Tsarist state. Yet the Orthodox Church continued to stress the religious foundations of that state. Thus, when we study the religious history of the West, we find that religion is connected in complex ways to human relatedness in all its manifold forms.

When we turn to China, we are immediately struck by the overwhelming presence of the social in all its forms, both *gemeinschaftlich* and *gesellschaftlich*. Yet this generalization needs to be tempered by three observations. (1) The dominant categories of sociopolitical thought in traditional China do not carry the ontic weight of the dominant categories of post-Enlightenment Western social thought. (2) In many ways individuals play a role of supreme importance in traditional Chinese high culture and even in the popular culture. (3) And both of these propositions are related to the fact that there did not occur the radical disjuncture between the cosmic and human realms which occurs in the post-Cartesian West. Without entering into the semantics of the word *religion*, the cosmos for the most part remained a source of religious-philosophic meaning and of ethical values in China.

There are problems involved in applying Western concepts to China, but for the purposes of this discussion I shall simply assume that they are usable. As already indicated, the Confucian view of the family as a *Gemeinschaft* seems to resonate remarkably with that of Tönnies. Both seemed to believe that the network of familial roles is based on a preestablished "natural" order. Both believed that these roles are governed by clear-cut norms of proper behavior, a behavior which in the Chinese case involved specific rituals and forms of behavior. The common values which bind the family do not primarily subserve other utilitarian or "functional" goals beyond the harmony and moral well-being of the family as a community. What is more, as in the case of Tönnies, the natural hierarchic and authoritarian basis of the family by no means derogates ideally from its communitarian harmony.

Yet while the Confucian family is in some sense a natural order,

the nature in question is by no means the same as Tönnies's nineteenth-century "scientific" biological nature. In point of origin,
the intense Chinese feeling for family has its roots in an age-old
orientation to what we call "ancestor worship." Tönnies expresses
the view that "in such natural relationships it is self-evident that
action will take place and be willed in accordance with the relationship,"[6] just as bees in a hive will naturally and automatically
behave in accordance with the norms inherent in their prepro-
grammed roles. Yet while the cosmically rooted and ordered rituals
and rules which govern proper Chinese role relationships include
the living family members, as well as the members who now abide
in the world beyond, the actual living human family members have
the fatal perverse human capacity to violate and transgress the
norms. Even in the earliest Confucian texts, the question is not,
What are the norms? but, How do we induce living human beings
to act according to those norms? Thus the *Analects* of Confucius
do not simply describe the rituals and rules governing proper family relations. They are largely concerned with the question of why
the families of Confucius' time had so grievously departed from
the norms, and how the norms could be reactualized. The answer
which seems to emerge is that the revival of the values of the family community could only be brought about by the moral self-
transformation of the individuals who comprise the community.
To be sure, those individuals who are able to achieve a high degree of moral self-improvement must express their moral achievement through the sacred framework of the network of family roles
and must carry out all the rituals which sustain these roles in a
reverential project. The *chün-tzu* or "noble man" does not prove
his individual moral spiritual quality by standing aside from his
familial roles but by the manner in which he plays his roles —
whether they be those of father, brother, or child, whether the
roles are those of a superordinate or subordinate position. The
familial *Gemeinde* as a social entity by no means has any automatic power to internalize its own norms into the members of the
community.

We are thus not surprised to find that a large part of *Analects*
is devoted not to discussions of the structures of the family as such —
or for that matter the structures of the political order — but rather
to the moral cultivation of the noble men (*chün-tzu*) who will

redeem society through the agency of their own individual self-cultivation.

The strain of Confucian thought which has become dominant in recent Chinese history and in neo-Confucianism should be described not only as ethical individualism but also as a cosmic-religious-mystical individualism. Here humanity relates to the ultimate cosmic source, Heaven or The Way, not primarily through the sacred institutions of the family or the polity but directly through the "heart" or soul of the individual. Within Confucianism this ethico-religious individualism is by no means antithetical to the communitarian or the sociopolitical. Yet compared to the drastic Hegelian-Marxist antithesis between the "isolated individual" and the "ensemble of social relations," the Confucian understanding places much more weight on the side of the role of individuals, even though these individuals are not isolated from the social; and less weight on the ontic claims made for the "ensemble of social relations" as a *Ding an sich*.

We have, of course, been speaking of ethical and religio-philosophic individualism within a broadly Confucian framework. The fact is that if one looks beyond this framework one can find even more radical varieties of this kind of religious individualism which eschew the very notion of redemption through the social, as in that strain in the Book of *Chuang-tzu* where we find a kind of aesthetic-mystical individualism which became completely unhinged from any exaltation of the communitarian or the sociopolitical.

To be sure, these individualistic strains in Chinese high culture have nothing to do with the individualism of human rights grounded in law, the individualism of the "economic man," the individualism of an aesthetic romanticism, or the individualism of "everyman." While these are doctrines of human nature which attribute to all humans the potentiality for moral self-cultivation and self-perfection, there is the expectation that only a vanguard will actually be capable of actualizing its moral potentiality. The vast majority of the people can not be expected to realize their moral potentialities, whether because of genetic limitations or, more significantly, because of an overwhelmingly unfavorable sociopolitical environment. Thus on one level society does in fact seem to be molded, not by a vanguard of superior individuals but by a kind of social determinism. Yet the social determinism in question reminds us of certain strains of eighteenth-century Enlightenment social thought rather than of nineteenth-century sociologism with its emphasis on the "system" as such. The families of the people have been effectively barred from realizing their communitarian ideals by the perversity and corruption of those individuals who control the political order. It is only when good and wise individuals create the appropriate environment that realization of the ideals is possible on the popular level.

These correlations inevitably turn our attention from the role of the family to the role of the political order in divine society. In the *Analects* we find a concern basically with two social structures: the family and the political order. Within the Confucian alternative, the family remains the paradigm *Gemeinschaft* par excellence, since the family is the first school of morality and also the true paradigm for the political order. It is to be noted that Confucian culture takes for granted from the outset that the family is not a self-sufficient, isolated community but part of a larger sociocultural order. Unlike the primitivist Taoism of the *Book of Lao-tzu*, the Confucius of the *Analects* accepts wholeheartedly the values of "higher civilization," including all the institutions of the political order. Indeed, while the origins of the moral lie in the ancestor-worshipping family, the flourishing of most families even in Confucius' view depends on the moral state of the political order. And yet, the idea that the state is based on the paradigm of the family *Gemeinde* remains, to use the words of Geertz in connection with Bali, "more than a passing metaphor, a statement of a political ideal"[7] which does in fact profoundly influence the course of history. While its influence has been profound for many in the field, including myself, the matter remains highly problematic. To many of us it would appear that the goal-oriented *gesellschaftlich* tendencies of large-scale organizations were not only present in the universal state of post-Ch'in empire but were already beginning to appear in the politics of Confucius' time. Indeed one might almost say that Confucianism represented an age-long sustained resistance to a tendency toward *gesellschaftlichkeit* in the nature of the state. Indeed, in the fourth and third centuries we have the emergence in China of a remarkable school of thought, known in the West as legalism, which explicitly rejected the Confucian family community as a model for the state and along with it repudiated the role of individual agency in transforming the state. It was a mode of thought which came as close as anything in the premodern world to an anticipation of Weber's conception of rational bureaucracy and even of legal rationality. The Confucian resistance was thus not simply the unconscious reaction of a backward "patrimonial bureaucracy," which could hardly have dreamt of anything like a Weberian *gesellschaftlich* rational bureaucracy. Nor can one say that the Confucian resistance, for good or ill, does not effectively check the march toward full rationalization and decisively shape the political culture.

As in the case of the family community, the flourishing of an exemplary polity depended wholly on the personal moral and intellectual quality of the individuals who filled the offices of the state and its bureaus (including the Emperor himself) rather than on the magical sacred qualities of the structures themselves, although these structures are both religiously grounded. None of this provided any infallible way of assuring that the best and the wisest would be brought to power, but neither did it suggest that the institutions could automatically transform the quality of their occupants. Throughout the course of Chinese history neither the literati nor the masses believed that fatherhood or emperorship could in any way cure the mediocrity and fallibility of actual fathers and emperors. In an ideal polity, such as that which presumably existed in the days of Yao, Shun, and Yu, the occupants of the throne were sage-kings who infused the ceremonial and political institutions of the state with the spirit of their sageliness. In later ages it was almost a cliche that this state of grace had long since departed. While the authority inherent in the hierarchic institutions of family and state was inviolable and awesome, and while its critics enjoyed no legally grounded protection against its arbitrary use, experience had long since proven that these *gemeinschaftlich* structures provided no guarantee against dismal corruption and perversion. Again, while the jurisdiction of state authority was all-encompassing, this did not imply a goal-oriented totalitarian control of every aspect of society. Just as in a family where actual fathers are ideal fathers, the harmony of the family is maintained, not by punitive coercive measures but by the spirit of ceremonial decorum which pervades family life; an ideal state does not have to intervene aggressively in every department of social and cultural life.

In conclusion, I have made these points about the applicability of the notion of community as *Gemeinschaft* to China not in order to idealize either the traditional Chinese family or the traditional Chinese polity. On the level of actuality, the arbitrary and despotic abuse of power and authority was certainly as much a fact of Chinese history as the history of any other of the "higher civilizations." I would simply suggest that if something like the notion of community is to be found, it does not have the ontic weight which it seems to have acquired in the modern West. The community as a social entity does not have the automatic power to instill its ideals into the members of the community. It is in fact easily corrupted, and it is by no means incompatible with a large degree of what might be called moral and religio-cosmic individualism. Indeed, the flourishing of a community depends on the moral quality of its constitutive members. There is no obligation to assume that any actual political regime embodies the ideality of an ideal community.

The latter point has a certain relevance to aspects of the contemporary situation in China. Does the Marxist-Leninist regime in China simply represent a continuity with the despotism of the Chinese past? While there are undoubtedly areas of continuity, I would suggest that the concept of a Marxist-Leninist party (whether it is thought of as *gemeinschaftlich* or *gesellschaftlich*) may owe much more to the polar extreme of Western sociologism than it does to the Chinese past. Presumably the Party incarnates the messianic ideality and infallibility which Marx believes to be immanent in the proletariat. As such its present leadership — whether it be embodied in one individual or in a group — virtually embodies the immanent wisdom and moral values assigned to the Party as a social entity. The opposition view that the emperor may be wearing no clothes is much more in keeping with some of the main tendencies of traditional thought.

NOTES

1. There are, to be sure, still mechanical-materialists who explain human beings wholly in terms of nonhuman cosmic causes, but they are a minority.

2. Karl Marx, *Die Frühschiften* (Stuttgart: Alfred Kröner, 1953), pp. 339–40.

3. A social system or formation is not only able to govern the behavior of all the individuals and groups which fall within its orbit. It is also able to generate within its "womb" the system which will succeed it.

4. Martin Buber, *Between Man and Man* (London: Routledge & Kegan Paul, 1949), p. 31.

5. Ferdinand Tönnies, *Community and Society (Gemeinschaft und Gesellschaft)*, ed. and trans. Charles P. Loomis (East Lansing, Mich.: Michigan State University Press, 1957), p. 25.

6. Ibid.

7. Clifford Geertz, *Interpretation of Cultures* (New York: Basic Books, 1973), ch. 14, "Person, Time, and Conduct in Bali."

8

Dignity in Difference:
Organic Realism and
the Quest for Community

HUSTON SMITH

AMERICAN SOCIAL PHILOSOPHY is built on a prospective idealism. "All people," we say, "are created equal." This really means that we intend to treat all people as equal before the law in certain fundamental respects, and to ensure equality of economic opportunity. None of this really happens as it is supposed to, but the cash value of this commitment is some protection against those oppressions that are based on race, class, creed, sex, and the like.[1]

The price we pay for the above is the unrealism of thinking that we all have equal gifts and callings — that anyone can grow up to be President. This we know is not true.

Idealism without Realism: Can It Work?

Can idealism, wedded to unrealism, work? Logically it seems unlikely, and empirically it looks like America is not working very well. Our idealistic preachments about equality and our political efforts to facilitate it do not prevent chief executive officers from receiving 192 times the salaries of their blue collar workers. Economic disparity is as great in America today as it was in the Europe that drove Marx to lock himself in the British Museum for forty years to search for a way out. The homeless increase in number, and parts of every major American city look more and more like Calcutta.

If idealism grounded in unrealism is not working and logically (it stands to reason) cannot work, perhaps we should attend to its unrealistic base. We have given the first two centuries of our republic to working on idealism. Perhaps it's time to think seriously about realism.

The Flight from Realism

The project faces odds because realism calls us to accountability. In asserting that there is a way things are, which way we either take into account or suffer the consequences, realism makes demands on us.[2] This is unattractive. We would rather have things our way, which is the half-noble, half-ridiculous idealistic dream. Scientists, in the fashion of settlers enlarging their forest clearings, push reality back and replace it with "virtual reality," a humanly devised environment in which the unattractive features of natural settings are removed.[3] Social scientists claim that "virtual reality" (in a different sense from the one just employed) already exists, it being the only reality we have. In this second sense reality is virtual in being a social construct, à la Berger and Luckmann's *Social Construction of Reality*. What we take for facts are actually artifacts. Philosophers distance reality by denying the existence of "essences." You can bump into an essence, but it's unpleasant to bump into things, so essences are dismissed as reifications. Efforts to come to grips with them are said to be prompted by naive (if not oppressive) epistemologies that turn on domineering notions like correspondence and reference. New age physics rejects realism by claiming that the world remains indeterminate until we call it into being by collapsing amorphous wave packets through experimental, superpositional interventions. What survives all this banishing of realism is a blizzard of deconstructed texts.

This essay targets for inspection the revolt against realism that is raging around us. Defining realism more or less commonsensically—there are things that are real; there is a way things are, whether we face up to that fact or not—I propose to table moral idealism until we examine the fixed pieces with which idealism must work. I am not abandoning idealism. My object is to move it into a setting which, being more realistic, promises greater success. My guiding metaphor is C. S. Peirce's idealistic drunk who careens out of a bar into a lamp post. What are the lamp posts that social theory must take into account? It is Peirce the realist, not Dewey and James as read romantically, who charts my course.

Toward Social Realism: Is Society Organic?

The realism I am after in this essay has to do with whether societies are organic or mechanical. Do they consist of interchangeable parts on the order of Adam Smith's economic human and John Locke's *tabula rasa*, or do the parts of a body politic differ as the organs of an animal body do? Are people basically alike, or constitutionally different? They are both, of course, but are their constitutional differences pronounced enough to require being taken into account by social theorists? By constitutional differences I am not thinking of physiological ones such as those that pertain to gender, coloration, and the like. Nor am I thinking of ethnic differences that stem from nurture rather than nature. My question is whether, alongside innate biological differences, there exist innate temperamental differences in people. Overlying human nature, are there human natures?

If there are, I shall table the question of their etiology. Astrologers invoke planetary conjunctions, Indians the karma of past lives, and there is the enduring puzzle of heredity's place in the picture. There is even the possibility that if societies are organic, they *create* differences in their constituents. This possibility runs counter to science's inclination to explain wholes in terms of their parts, but evidence is mounting for a supplementing causation that proceeds from whole to part. By means we have no clue to, bodies produce different kinds of cells according to whether they are parts of liver, fingernail, hair, or brain—this despite the fact that all of the cells possess the same DNA. Perhaps societies possess a similar power to decree that their members too will differ, while remaining at the same time human.

This possibility is important enough to warrant a second paragraph. Certain animal kingdoms clearly instance the power of whole over part. An entomologist, noticing that some of the ants in the colony he was studying were industrious while others were lazy, separated the two groups. Half of the lazy ants became industrious, and half of the industrious ants grew lazy. Perhaps ant

colonies require a certain quota of industrious ants to endure and
have devised ways of producing them when they are needed. More
startling is what happens in schools of the brightly colored fish,
scalefin anthias. When a male dies, the largest female in the school
changes sex to take its place. Within two weeks her color changes
from orange-red to the male coloration of violet-purple. Gonads
appear, and "her" behavior transforms into that of a fully functioning male.[4] One of the arguments that environmentalists mount
for protecting endangered species is the possibility that they may
be "organs of the ecosystem" that service the system in ways that
are important but as yet undiscovered.

With these passing observations I drop the question of how,
if innate temperamental differences do exist, they get fixed in place.
For the exploratory purposes of this essay I shall adopt the working hypothesis that they *do* exist; Jean-Paul Sartre encourages me
here when, on his own and different topic, he proposes as the
subtlest form of anti-Semitism the assumption of non-Jews that
Jews are just like themselves. Deploying this hypothesis, I shall ask,
first, what the most important differences of the sort I have targeted are, and thereafter what their import for community building might be. Because the premise is unpopular, I bolster my
courage by explaining why I adopt it. Because innate differences
provide the obvious rationale for oppression — master over slave
in whatever guise — it disturbs us to consider even the possibility
that they exist. This keeps us from examining, clear-eyed and open-
mindedly, the facts of the matter. Disjoined from realism, moral
idealism is handicapped. I proceed now to suggest what the innate temperamental differences in the human species might be.

Toward a Socially Useful Characterology

"What's your type?" is a popular parlor game, but more. The
move to discover oneself, by discovering things one shares with certain of one's fellows but not all, seems to be a universal compulsion. When the identifying traits are taken as constitutional, they
help to define the self and establish for it a trajectory. Astrology
is the oldest and most universal characterology. In the West it was
supplemented by the typology — dating from Empedocles, Hippoc-
rates, and Galen — that linked four basic temperaments (sanguine,

phlegmatic, choleric, and melancholic) to their respective natural elements (air, water, fire, and earth) and bodily humors (blood, phlegm, yellow bile, and black bile). Modern psychology enters the act by using characterology as a diagnostic tool. Freud classified his patients as hysterical, obsessive-compulsive, and schizoid, toward which types even "normals" incline. Jung began by dividing people into extroverts and introverts and went on to overlay this dichotomy with his quaternity of thinking, feeling, sensing, and intuitive types.

This sample of classifications that have been ventured gets us into my subject, but it does no more than that because it is not clear where they point politically. They may be important for self-understanding and clinical treatment, but these are of psychological moment whereas the book this essay is written for addresses the issue of community. For Western characterologies that have social ramifications I shall mention Plato's and Saint-Simon's before turning to the Hindu varnic scheme which will provide a bridge to my own typology.

Plato saw people as appetitive, spirited, and rational, and designed his Republic around the three classes — workers, guardians, and rulers — that the types constituted. His picaresque, modern utopian successor, Count Claude Saint-Simon, accepted Aristotle's premise that people desire to express their intrinsic and immutable aptitudes and went on to argue that this desire is more basic than the wish to be equal with others. Administration — Saint-Simon eschewed the word *government* — makes trouble for itself if it does not take into account the natural differences that people seek to express. Like the mid-twentieth-century psychologist William Sheldon, he believed that temperamental differences derive from differences in physique, and classified people according to whether their hearts, their heads, or their muscles predominated. Heart people were sensitive, intuitive, and visionary; head people — scientists, by his definition — were analytic, rational, and practical; and muscular types excelled in physical activity. For society, these differences dictated that visionaries should be planners who point the direction in which society should move; scientists (the rational, analytic type) should figure out how to get there; and people of muscular physique and disposition should implement the steps the scientists propose.

The Hindu *varnas*, it seems to me, "cut closer to the joints" of the body politic than do either of the foregoing typologies. I realize that in venturing this I run the risk of losing my audience, for the caste system was based on the *varna* theory, and feelings against caste now run so high that to suggest that it might have been right in any respect is likely to bring conversation to a halt. But if I say that my interest here is in the human differences the *varnas* identify, not what the *Dharma-śāstras* and *Laws of Manu* did with those differences, perhaps there is point in continuing.

To get to the heart of the four varnic types I shall quote Frithjof Schuon. The quotation is longer than is usually appropriate in an essay, but I enter it because the *varnas* come closest to the typology I shall myself propose, and Schuon draws profiles of its four types with an insight I find unrivaled.

> The fundamental tendency in a man is connected with his feeling or consciousness of what is "real." For the *brahmin* — the purely intellectual, contemplative and sacerdotal type — it is the changeless, the transcendent, which is real; in his innermost heart he does not "believe" either in "life" or in "earth"; something in him remains foreign to change and to matter; broadly speaking such is his inner disposition — what might be called his "imaginative life"— whatever may be the personal weaknesses by which it is obscured. The *ksattriya* — the knightly type — has a keen intelligence, but it is turned towards action and analysis rather than towards contemplation and synthesis; his strength lies especially in his character; he makes up for the aggressiveness of his energy by his generosity and for his passionate nature by his nobility, self-control, and greatness of soul. For this human type it is action that is real, for it is by action that things are determined, modified and ordered; without action there is neither virtue nor honour nor glory. In other words the *ksattriya* believes in the efficacy of action rather than in the fatedness of a given situation: he despises the slavery of facts and thinks only of determining their order, of clarifying a chaos, of cutting Gordian knots. Thus, just as for the *brahmin* all is changeful and unreal except the Eternal and whatever is attached to It — truth, knowledge, contemplation, ritual, the Way — so for the *ksat-*

triya all is uncertain and peripheral except the constants of his *dharma* — action, honour, virtue, glory, nobility — on which for him all other values depend. The perspective can be transposed onto the religious plane without any essential change in its psychological quality.

For the *vaisya* — the merchant, the peasant, the artisan, the man whose activities are directly bound up with material values not merely *de facto* and accidentally but by virtue of their nature — it is riches, security, prosperity, and well-being that are real; in his instinctive life other values are secondary and in his innermost heart he does not "believe" in them; his imagination expands on the plane of economic stability, of the material perfection of work and the return it yields, and when this is transposed onto the religious plane it becomes exclusively a perspective of accumulating merit with a view to posthumous security. Externally this mentality is analogous to that of the *brahmin* by reason of its static and pacific character; but it is remote from the mentality both of the *brahmin* and the *ksattriya* because of a certain pettiness of the intelligence and will; the *vaisya* is clever and possesses common sense, but he lacks specifically intellectual qualities and also chivalrous virtues, idealism in the higher sense of the term. . . .

The "twice-born" (*dvija*), namely, the three castes of which we have spoken, might be defined as a spirit endowed with a body, and the *sudra* who represents the fourth caste, as a body endowed with human consciousness; in fact the *sudra* is the man who is properly qualified only for manual work of a more or less quantitative kind and not for work demanding greater initiative and more complex attitudes; for this human type, which is still more widely separated from the preceding types than is the *vaisya* from the noble castes, it is bodily things that are real; it is eating and drinking which in this case strictly constitutes happiness, these and their psychological concomitances; in the innate perspective of the *sudra*, in his "heart," all that lies outside the realm of bodily satisfaction smacks of luxury, not to say of illusion, or in any case seems something "alongside" of what his imagination takes for reality, namely the satisfaction of immediate physical needs. It might be objected that the knightly type is also one who enjoys, but this is not the point; here the question is above all the psychological function of enjoyment, the part it plays in an assemblage of compossibles; the *ksattriya* readily turns poet or aesthete; he lays very little stress on matter as such. The central and at the same time elementary place held by enjoyment in the innate perspective of the *sudra* explains his often carefree, dissipated and "momentary" character through which he rejoins, by a curious inverted analogy, the spiritual *sannyasi* who likewise lives in the moment, does not think of the morrow and wanders without apparent object; but the *sudra* is too passive in relation to matter to be able to govern himself and therefore remains dependent on a will other than his own; his virtue is fidelity, or a kind of massive rightness, no doubt dense but also simple and intelligible, and therefore also worthy of respect, a fact which is sometimes forgotten.[5]

So much in this description feels right to me that I do not know whether the characterology I shall now myself set forth differs from it in substance or merely in formulation. Be this as it may, the typology itself is as follows.

The Basic Human Differences

People differ most importantly — this is the possibility I wish to set forth — in the size of the worlds they inhabit.[6]

The gradations in those worlds have their precursors in subhuman nature. Inanimate matter has no "world." Its total passivity is equivalent to the absence of an existential world to engage with. A plant has a "world" of sorts — a bit of soil, water, air, light, and a few other things to work with — a world that is limited to its biological needs. The animal world is incomparably greater and richer. Though it is still biologically governed, it exceeds the plant's world by dint of the animal's mobility and curiosity.

The human world is greater and richer still. Traditional philosophies go so far as to designate the human self the *capax universi*, capable of bringing the entire universe into its experience. This brings me at once to the governing principle in my typology.

The human mind may in principle be capable of bringing the whole of reality under review, but actual minds realize that possibility to different degrees. "The world spreads out on either side / No wider than the heart is wide," Edna St. Vincent Millay observed,[7] and hearts and minds extend to different extents. They thereby stake out for themselves worlds of varying sizes, we can add, and this provides me with the measure for my classification. Four of these sizes reappear with such regularity as to suggest a typology that is at least heuristically useful, if there are not in fact "quantum jumps" between the types that replicate on the human plane the gradations that divide the mineral, vegetable, and animal kingdoms. The height of a life, I am suggesting, turns on the height — and length and breadth and depth as well, for spatial metaphors only hint — of its lived world: the world it inhabits existentially.

This proposal must face the objection that it is hierarchical and therefore elitist, so to try to offset that objection let me register two points and follow them with two rhetorical questions. (a) The final worth of persons — their place in the eyes of God; the complete arc of their lives which could conceivably stretch through a number of lifetimes; or the way they all embody the *imago dei*, *Atman*, or Buddha-nature — is not in question. It is evidential features in a single lifetime that are under review. (b) Not all hierarchies are oppressive. People can be ranked on a scale of compassion as readily as on any other scale. The two questions that follow these two points are the following: (a) Once the issue of people's final worth is bracketed (as per the first point above), is it not the case that in almost every proximate respect — athletic prowess, artistic talent, virtually any capacity — people are manifestly unequal? (b) Would it not be a disservice to deprive people of role models they could look up to and virtues to which they might aspire? Both disservices would follow if hierarchies of worth are disallowed.

If these considerations legitimize not just horizontal classifications but also ones that are vertical in registering gradations of worth, I can return to my proposal that we identify people by the size of the worlds they inhabit. The standard measures of size are time and space, and the four worlds I shall identify as housing my four personality types are positioned on their continuums. Spatially the world of my first type of person does not extend very much beyond the reach of his or her senses. The question, Is it real? translates into, Can you see or touch it? Temporally this type is glued, pretty much, to the here and now—the present. These people have short attention spans; they have difficulty denying themselves present gratifications for the sake of future rewards. Spatially the second type's world expands to include family, friends, and other face-to-face associates, while temporally it extends to cover the lifespans of these personal acquaintances. The third type's world balloons to include spatially the entire planet, and temporally all human history. Such people are moved to mount rescue missions for boat people in Cambodia and famine victims in Ethiopia; for the lives of all people, through the simple fact that they are human, impact this third type to some degree. As for the world of the fourth type, it sheds all boundaries. Spatially it extends to the infinite, and temporally to the eternal.

When I speak of the four types as inhabiting these four respective worlds, I mean that what each takes to be "really real" lies within the world that was specified. In current vernacular, each targeted world is, for the type in question, "where it's at."

Needing names for the four types and wanting to move quickly to the social relevance of this typology, I shall designate them by the occupations that are likely to interest them. In the order of the above listing, I shall call them (without enthusiasm; surely better names could be found) workers, providers, shapers, and guides. In conjunction with their types of work, I shall mention the raw materials each is drawn toward working with.

workers.   Everyone works, but the eyes of this first type of person are on the work itself rather than its product, which is likely to belong to others. I have suggested that the lived world of this first type does not extend far beyond its body, and as a consequence they tend to associate work with what their bodies do. Manual laborers fall into this class. To say that hired hands do also is to turn to the temporal gauge. As these people have a short attention span, they are not adept at planning their lives far in advance and tend to benefit by supervision. Setting few long-term goals for themselves, they take jobs that turn up when they need money. If those jobs fold they look for others, and if a surplus accrues they are apt to stop working until their money runs out. We do not like to think that there are people of this first type, but we must remember: the question this essay presses is not how we would like things to be, but the way they actually are.

providers.   Having a longer time sense, work for the second type of person aims at its object, which is usually a material artifact of some sort — food, clothing, shelter, whatever. The raw material here is likewise some form of matter, be it wood, stone, metal, seed and soil, or another natural resource.

The raw material for *shapers*, by contrast, is people in the aggregate, the human community which through fine-tuning or revolutionary overhaul they want to shape to perfection, or as close thereto as is possible. Whether they are politicians or administrators, social theorists or social activists, the eyes of this third type are on the human potential considered not individually but collectively. They work on institutional structures that regulate human interactions. If a provider creates a company, it will be for the tangible product it makes and distributes. Shapers — lawyers are included in this type — are more occupied with the human dynamics that are involved. How can the doings of people be orchestrated so as to support one another, not cancel each other out?

Finally, *guides.* This type is most interested in truth and understanding — for its intrinsic beauty in the first instance, but also practically as a beacon for life. Their raw materials are intangible — ideas, values, beauty, things of the spirit in general.

If it is to be just, a differentiated society would need to reward each type in proportion to the services it renders. As all four types of service are needed they should be rewarded equally. But the rewards must differ in kind, for the types value different things. *Providers*, being primarily interested in material things, should be rewarded in the coin of their greatest delight — money and the things it can buy. *Shapers* are more invested in human relationships, and as they want to influence those relationships, let the power to do so — social power (political, administrative) at whatever level — be their reward. Neither wealth nor power interests *guides* most — if they do the individuals are wrongly typed — so the reward due them is the respect forthcoming from the other types for being to appreciable degree beyond such things and vectored by "the higher things of life"— things that are intangibles. The respect could be genuine, for the other types vaguely sense that higher values exist, even though they don't place them first in their lives.

This leaves the *workers*, who in every society seem to be the least advantaged. In the present typology too they would have less wealth, power, and prestige than the other three classes. But one not negligible reward would be theirs, namely, freedom. An honest day's work would be expected of them in return for an honest day's pay — a decent standard of living. But when 5:00 came they would be through. There would be no homework to turn to after dinner, no long-term responsibilities to occupy their minds in their off hours. They would not be indentured to a single occupational slot for their working years; indeed, work would consume a smaller portion of their lives, probably a more humane portion, given our workaholic society. With the possible exception of the most advanced *guides*, they would be freer than the other types to live fully in the present. Even in our existing society, hippies and "mountain people" in regions like Big Sur enjoy some of the freedom of India's *sannyasis*.

The Existing Alternative

All of this is worked out so sketchily that I do not want to rest my case on it; perhaps even the four divisions I have suggested are not the right ones. What I do hold to is the prospect of there being a better way to organize society than our present one, a way that takes seriously the possibility that people are not totally malleable and that respects their innate differences.

If my suggested blueprint seems fantastic, we should not overlook how fantastic — unfunctional — our current, unitrack system is. It is, on balance and for all practical purposes, a single-track system that types people in the same way and expects them to compete in the same race — the *vaisya* race in which the standard of living and upward mobility are measured by material possessions. In the society we have, "What is he or she worth?" comes close to being read as "How much does he or she have?" More than by anyone else, this single-track society was fixed in place by the half-genius, half-lunatic John Locke. His genius side needs no arguing, for one does not assemble what Robert Bellah suggests is perhaps the most powerful ideology ever forged if one is not in some way brilliant. As for his lunatic side, are we really to believe that the mind is a *tabula rasa* that can be imprinted in any way we please? This is the myth of a human sameness, indefinitely malleable, that this essay has targeted for inspection. On the foundations of this sameness, Locke projected a government that would, above all else, protect people's right to amass property; it is common knowledge that in the Preamble to the Constitution of the United States, the "inalienable rights" that all are said to be created with were initially listed as "life, liberty, and the acquisition of property." Jürgen Habermas has warned of "the colonization of the life world" by what he calls the System, a collusion of government and the market economy, and what I have written can be seen as an attempt to take seriously his warning.

If people are constitutionally different, the System does well by those who share its values — the economic values of the *vaisya* type as suggested above. Others, whose values lie elsewhere because their worlds are of different proportions, find themselves homeless. Welfare if not personal acquisition may raise a roof over their heads, but their souls are out in the streets. Other talents for the marketplace may be lacking in them, but their chief handicap is that their hearts are not fully there; they lack "the fire in the belly" for economic competition that Walter Mondale in the end concluded he lacked for politics. Here are some of the things our monorail society deprives whole sectors of the population of:

a. Respect. They have it if they are high (or moving up) on the social scale, which in our System is the economic ladder. But what resources for self-respect do we offer those on its lower rungs? Or have we drifted off again into daydreams of an egalitarian society in which there is no top or bottom because there is no social scale?

b. Guidelines for vocational choice. The days of following an ancestral line in one's occupation are over. In its place we have the yuppie model and vocational aptitude tests. For the rest, people are left to themselves to figure out how to deal with a bewildering array of vocational options.

c. The sense of calling, or vocation in the true sense of that word; the feeling that one is doing what one is cut out to do, and valued because society recognizes that what one is doing is vital to its well-being — as indispensable as are kidneys (as much as brains and hearts) to a body's well-being. Our society has no operative concept of sacred duty, one's *dharma*, as the Hindus call it. It is in the human makeup to want to help, but one wonders if all our volunteer welfare programs, admirable as they are in their own way, contribute a fraction as much to our corporate well-being as would our regular occupations if they were performed conscientiously and in accord with guidelines we took seriously. In my typology the guideline for *workers* has already been noted; it is an honest day's work for an honest day's pay. The rule for *providers* would be to do what they could to improve the material standard of living for society as a whole. (The total absence of such a moral rule today is illustrated by the recent savings and loan scandal wherein those who knew how to maneuver the intricacies of our economy used that knowledge to transfer an estimated $500 billion from taxpayers' pockets into their own.)[8] The responsibility that *shapers* would acknowledge would be to create institutions that enable human energies to reinforce one another instead of canceling each other out; in current parlance, to maximize win-win situations. *Guides* would try to demonstrate, not just say, where life's final good resides. On the social plane, this good consists in finding the well-being of the part (the individual) through the well-being of the whole (family, community, nation, and world).

d. Finally, someone to look up to. Well-intentioned though they are, critics of hierarchies overlook this human need. Without role models we are without handholds as we try to scale life's cliff. In a typology calibrated by the size of the worlds people live in, each type can to some degree sense (and feel drawn to) the world that is immediately above it. They genuinely respect those who inhabit it. Thus *workers* can respect *providers* and their talents for managing their lives; they can even wish (with parts of their being) to be like them. A comparable, one-step, upturned gaze of aspiration characterizes the other types, with *guides* looking upward to God.

Summary

As I have indicated, the characterology I have outlined is negotiable. What I cannot get away from, and hence am not prepared to back away from, is my sense that society is organic. If it is, until we face up to this fact and identify its principal organs — metaphor, here, for the distinct human temperaments that comprise the body politic — we should ask ourselves seriously how far we think our idealism can carry us toward a just and true community.

NOTES

1. I am indebted to the editor of this volume, Leroy Rouner, for guiding a mass of inchoate thoughts on my subject to whatever coherence the essay achieves. Professor Jackson Crittenden of the Department of Political Science at Arizona State University also made helpful suggestions. Neither is responsible for the final product.

2. Samuel Alexander's observation on this point remains perhaps the best succinct one that has been made: "The temper of realism is to deanthropomorphize. . . . So natural is the self-flattering habit of supposing that mind . . . is in some special sense the superior of physical things . . . that realism in questioning its prerogative appears to some to degrade the mind. . . . [Yet] realism strips mind of its pretensions but not of its value or greatness. Realism is the democratic spirit in metaphysics, and if it dethrones the mind, it recognizes mind as chief in the world it knows" ("The Basis of Realism," in *Realism and the Background of Phenomenology*, ed. R. M. Chisholm [Glencoe, Ill.: Free Press, 1960], p. 186).

3. See Robert Wright, "Virtual Reality," *The Sciences* 7, no. 6 (November/December 1987).

4. See Joseph Levine, "Pecking Order and Sexual Politics," *The Smithsonian* 21, no. 4 (July 1990): 90–91.

5. Frithjof Schuon, *Castes and Races* (Middlesex, England: Perennial Books, 1982), pp. 11–14. A supporting justification for entering a quotation of this length is that this book had a limited printing and is not readily accessible.

6. Having completed this essay, I come upon another sentence by Frithjof Schuon that suggests that my typology is basically an extension of the one he depicted. "Psychologically speaking," Schuon writes, "a natural caste is a cosmos; men live in different cosmoses according to the

reality on which they are centered, and it is impossible for the lower really to understand the higher, for he who really understands 'is' what he understands" (ibid., p. 33).

7. Edna St. Vincent Millay, "Renascence."

8. See Michael Thomas, "The Greatest American Shambles," *New York Review of Books*, 31 January 1991.

PART III

The Future
of Community

9

Religion and
the Quest for Community

PATRICK J. HILL

MUCH OF THE PHILOSOPHY OF COMMUNITY focuses on the reconciliation of liberal conceptions of the individual with the *desiderata* of communal life. My focus is a macroscopic version of that philosophical reconciliation. I am concerned with the reconciliation of diverse communities with human and planetary solidarity. I will focus particularly on interactions among diverse religious groups. How have the relationships among religions been conceived, and how might they be rethought?

I

By the quest for community I mean the variety of attempts to overcome the isolation, disregard, caricature, or hostility among individuals or groups, by discovering, proposing, or establishing commonalities upon which to build the more or less frequent and sustained interaction of one sort or another which will likely be called a community.

But what do we mean by the concept of community? George Hibbert once distinguished ninety-four different meanings of the concept in sociology alone. When one adds to the sociological usage the philosophical ones, each of which tends to be idiosyncratic, we have a highly ambiguous concept. What John Herman Randall observed about the concept of philosophy seems to me equally true of the concept of community: that every definition is only a definition of a particular kind.

Nevertheless, the word *community* is unusual in that its connotations are so unqualifiedly positive. As Raymond Williams noted:

> *Community* can be the warmly persuasive word to describe an existing set of relationships, or the warmly persuasive word to describe an alternative set of relationships. What is most important, perhaps, is that unlike all other terms of social organization (state, nation, society, etc.) it seems never to be given any positive opposing or distinguishing term.[1]

This aura is particularly strong in some Jewish and Christian traditions in which we are fulfilled as human beings to the extent that we work with the loving action of God to create a universal community. In these traditions self-centeredness is often uncritically conflated with immorality, and community building with morality or holiness.

Rather than supposing community to be an absolute good and the quest for community a moral struggle against the evils of self-centered individualism, I see two sets of values in conflict: that set of values associated with the still incomplete revolution of democracy (freedom, self-determination, individuality, participation, diversity, dissent, mobility, privacy, and even anonymity); and another set of values most pervasively embodied in the preindustrial *Gemeinschaften* (loyalty, fidelity, rootedness, solidarity, public responsibility, neighborliness, communication, and civic pride). The democratic values, philosophically speaking, made the *Gemeinschaften* unworkable; but that does not mean that individuality and diversity are evil or even inherently immoral. All it means is that we are in need of different communal forms, far more sensitive to diversity and participation than were the *Gemeinschaften*. Community builders condemn themselves to failure if they do not realize that for good historical and psychological reasons many people perceive efforts to establish community as an inherently undemocratic notion, a thrust that is necessarily homogenizing and often hierarchical.

Because of the ambiguous character of the concept and because of its emotional freight, I have taken to substituting for the concept of community the emotionally unfreighted and purposefully general concept of "structures of association." Like a good pragmatist, I regard these structures as more or less appropriate to the context and the purpose for which they are built. If, for example, one is attempting to build a voluntary professional society to enable people who *already* share a culture and a set of values, one would include a nonhierarchical governance, a style of interaction, and a frequency of meeting appropriate to that purpose and context. If, however, one is attempting to build a community wherein values and culture are *not* shared at the outset, the structures appropriate to that task will be quite different.

II

Diversity is the key issue here, and I suggest four dimensions of what it means to respect diversity.

A. *Valuing Diversity*

The first concerns the comparative value of diversity and commonality. We will make no progress in forging a concept of community appropriate to the diversity of the contemporary world unless we abandon the notion that what is common is inherently more valuable than what is diverse. It is that assumption which has led many people to characterize the notion of community as essentially illiberal if not totalitarian. The messy historical truth is that sometimes what is common is more important for some purposes than what is diverse, and sometimes the opposite is true. Moreover, even when the case seems strongest for the greater importance of what is held in common, it will often seem otherwise to other groups.

Within the context of democratic values, however, we should be willing to respect diversity by regarding it as a resource and not a defect. Unanimous votes are good news for the recipient victors but not for the long-term health of a democracy. A diversity in a gene pool is a strength, not a weakness. Symphonic music is the richer for the different sounds of the piccolo and the flute. Sameness or unanimity, depending on the context, is often a threat, a weakness, or a bore.

B. The Ecology of Community

The second way in which diversity is respected is by examining the consequences of creating and sustaining particular communities. I call this inquiry the ecology of community.[2] Relative to the aura surrounding the quest for community, this inquiry has the effect of desacralizing the effort. The ecology of community has three fundamental concerns:

1. Understanding the genesis and decay of communities. Under what circumstances do people come to feel and to perceive that what they have in common is as important or less important than their differences? We can observe that phenomenon happening today in the European Common Market countries and (in the other direction) in the dissolution of the Soviet Union.
2. The study of criteria for evaluating communities. John Dewey, I believe, is the only philosopher of recent years who evolved such explicit criteria. He proposed two. The first was the number and variety of the interests consciously shared by the group. The second was the fullness and freedom of the interplay with other communities.[3] Such criteria cannot be neutral. Dewey's criteria reflected his primary commitment to growth. My criterion, namely, the consequences for sustaining conversations of respect in a diverse world, reflects value judgments generated by democracy and the environmental crisis. The criterion is not less important for being so situated.
3. The overall consequences, besides the formation and sustaining of community, of this or that particular community. A fundamental principle of ecology is that it is impossible to do merely one thing. The ecology of community studies the consequences additional to the prima facie noble intent of building and sustaining community.

Many who seek to build community believe that the quest for any kind of community that is not blatantly inhumane is good. The isolation of lives in the advanced industrial democracies makes it possible to believe that wherever two or three (whether individuals or groups) are gathered in some kind of fellowship or shared activity, there is cause for jubilation.

An examination of the full consequences of the building and sustaining of particular communities would ask many questions, including: Does this merger consolidate or distribute the control of whatever resources or authority were held before the action? Does this new formation improve or worsen the plight of those not part of the community? Are the people whom the community serves becoming more dependent or more self-reliant? Will dissent-ing or voice-finding movements be more or less enabled? Is there more or less local control, demeaning labor, unemployment, re-gard for the marginalized? Is the condition or participation of all women and of men of color improved or worsened?

Any quest for community is a quest for a particular kind of community to include particular people. While there is surely value in Christian-Buddhist dialogue and experiments in living, for ex-ample, there are chasms as large within Christianity itself. One can surely wonder if the poor of the world and the endangered species of the planet would not be better off if Christian ecumen-ism were more focused on a dialogue with liberation theologians and on North-South issues in general. The same is true of the fun-damental critique of Christianity originating with feminism or from within the environmental movement. The worth of a particular quest for community cannot be separated from the consequences of sustaining one community at the expense of another.

We need to become as observant and critical about the quest for community in the reconciliation of separate churches, for ex-ample, or in a neighborhood association, as we are about the merger of two large newspapers in our city, or about the purchase of Mobil by British Petroleum. On a full grid of the values important in a democratic society, are the consequences by and large positive or not?

C. Valuing Separateness

A third and related point concerns the respect which a demo-cratic society ought to accord to separateness, to the periodic with-drawals of groups or individuals from a larger community. Again the respect in question is not merely one of tolerance, but of nurturance and celebration.

Those who have participated in any attempt to define a new identity recognize the need for isolation from at least the dominating other and perhaps from all but those of an extreme likemindedness. In that isolation one defines a different agenda, and gains support and time and opportunities to create without the distraction of the other's incomprehension, impatience, curiosity, and judgment. The isolation is, at least temporarily, a source of creativity and vitality. Despite the importance in many contexts of what we all share, there is another equally important religious imperative. Rosemary Ruether has recently written about the separatist needs of women:

> Women in contemporary churches are suffering from linguistic deprivation and eucharistic famine. They can no longer nurture their souls in alienating words that ignore or systematically deny their existence. They are starved for the words of life, for symbolic forms that fully and wholeheartedly affirm their personhood and speak truth about the evils of sexism and the possibilities of a future beyond patriarchy. They desperately need primary communities that nurture their journey into wholeness, rather than constantly negating and thwarting it.[4]

In a democratic society the search for commonality must celebrate these newly separating "primary communities." They are to be encouraged because our commonality will eventually be enriched by their exploration.[5]

D. Conversations of Respect

Fourth, we need standards of conversation which respect and contribute to the sustaining of diversity. These are not the only worthwhile conversations. There are others wholly inside a set of shared boundaries; and there are thousands of motivations for conversations (among them outright playfulness) and thousands of purposes (among them political recruitment) which are unlike the conversations of respect I am about to describe.

Conversations of respect between diverse communities are

characterized by intellectual reciprocity. They are ones in which the participants expect to learn nonincidental things and expect to change at least intellectually as a result of the encounter. Such conversations are not animated by, nor do they result in, mere tolerance of the preexisting diversity, for political or ethical reasons. In such conversations, the participant does not treat the other as an illustration of a truth already fully possessed by oneself. There is no will to incorporate the other in any sense into one's belief system. In such conversations one participant does not presume that the relationship is one of teacher to student, of parent to child, of developed to underdeveloped. The participants are colearners.

Not all interdisciplinary conversations, to be sure, are respectful, but in genuinely respectful conversations, each disciplinary participant is aware at the outset of the incapacity of his or her own discipline to answer the question that is being asked. Each participant is aware of her or his partiality and of the need for the other. One criterion of the genuineness of the subsequent conversation is the transformation of each participant's understanding or definition of the question.

This definition of a conversation of respect may strike many as too demanding, uncritical, or relativistic; for it seems to suggest that the respect easily acknowledged as appropriate to conversations between Christians and Buddhists or between Christians and Jews is also appropriate to conversations between modern theologies and fundamentalists, pantheists, and other local and tribal religions. I have three brief responses to this concern. First, I remind you that I do not regard these conversations which cross religious boundaries as the only conversations worth having. Nor do I expect them to be the prime arena in which issues of social justice are pursued. The second brief comment is this. I do not believe that conversations of respect are or ought always to be possible, if only because of the aforementioned rhythms of separatist development. I am defining what such conversations would need to be like, when they are possible, if they are going to contribute intellectually to a sense shared across theological boundaries of an intellectual and theological dimension of human solidarity. I do not suppose that human solidarity cannot be achieved without this theological dimension, nor do I suppose that a contribution from organized religion or of humankind depends on the preexistence of such theological conversations or vision. To think of these conversations as prerequisite to the advancing of human solidarity would be to overemphasize the role of shared belief in generating and sustaining a sense of community. Third, in view of the collapse of Enlightenment values, the crisis of the planetary environment, and the many critiques of universalism, the reluctance of modernized theologies to converse with communities with preindustrial values ought to be considerably less than it was a quarter of a century ago. The deep distrust of modernity for everything which originated prior to the sixteenth century is no longer something which can be taken for granted.[6]

III

My definition of a conversation of respect requires a crossing of that "theological Rubicon" on the shores of which Hans Küng and other inclusivists have been encamped for several years. It requires, however we ground it philosophically and theologically, that we grant to religions other than our own an interdependent validity.[7]

Many alternatives exist, far more respectful than those of historical Christianity, to ground the validity of the world's diverse religions. Space permits just three brief observations:

A. For the ecology of community the sameness or difference of world religions is not an objective property of religions. The question for the ecology of community is the perceived significance of commonalities and differences. Under what conditions, asks the ecology of community, might previously distinct religions come to perceive that what they have in common is more significant to them than what they do not have in common?

B. The assessment of the usefulness of these frameworks for sustaining conversations of respect is in large measure an empirical question. Responses may vary with historical circumstances and with psychological types and cognitive styles. For persons raised in the exclusivist framework of Roman Catholicism, the perception of recurring themes in all religions may be as liberating as it was for Joseph Campbell. Those fascinated by the variety of human cultures may be more attracted to the relativism of Troeltsch. No general statement, I believe, could be adequate to the immense variety of starting points, cognitive styles, and historical circumstances.

C. Third, and of most general relevance to the philosophy of community: while the discernment of sameness in diverse religions obviously has functioned and can still function for some in a manner that sustains conversations of respect, I am bothered by what sometimes appears to be a conflation of understanding with assimilation. In the early stages of the decade-long dialogue between Thomas Merton and D. T. Suzuki, the former at least seemed overjoyed to discover similarities between the concepts of spiritual poverty and emptiness in Zen and the purity of heart and humility of the Desert Fathers. Merton slipped at times into supposing that he understood Suzuki because an idea in Zen seemed to resemble something he had encountered in Christianity. Merton seemed unable to say for many years anything like "The insights of Zen are quite different from ours and they are worth our attention."

What is missing in interreligious dialogue relative to my paradigm of conversations of respect is, of course, a sense of inadequacy or partiality, a sense of genuine need of the diverse other in order to accomplish some desired objective. Though the exceptions are numerous and unavoidable, religion and even theology have frequently defined themselves as providing complete answers to many of life's most gnawing questions. In certain contexts, such confidence may have been and may still be justified. It was not obvious until very recently that the religions of the world qua religions have ever experienced a theological or spiritual need for each other.

The closest parallel to my paradigm is the emergence in the Christian theology of religions of the theocentric model. This model, as I interpret it, has the potential to refocus religious attention away from comparatively familiar revealers and mediators toward the not fully known God. To the extent that the object of religious study or devotion is that unknown or still self-revealing God, the various religions of the world might be drawn upon as differing and perhaps complementary perspectives on our changing spiritual quest. Religions of the world might then be seen, not as varying perspectives on the same experience, but as different clusters of spiritual values appropriate to changing circumstances. In time, individuals might feel as comfortable as Raimundo Panikkar or Wilfred Cantwell Smith in drawing upon different religions for different spiritual purposes. Whole cultures faced with their irrelevance to a crisis like planetary endangerment might turn for help to cultures whose religions are based on different spiritual values, for example, living in harmony with nature. The differences, in this perspective, are resources for us all but only as we are able to perceive other religions as related to our spiritual quest.

Another approach comes from liberation theologians who ground interreligious cooperation in shared tasks like the elimination of world hunger or the saving of the endangered planet. Two important observations need to be made about this approach. First, from a doctrinal standpoint it is an indirect approach. While some theologians might feel this a shortcoming, the approach seems to me to create the possibility of dissolving caricatures, of situating doctrinal issues in larger contexts of spiritual values, and, in time, of perceiving similarities and differences less rigidly.[8]

The second observation is the more important. There are thousands of worthwhile tasks and hundred of urgent ones concerning which diverse religions might cooperate. The crucial question is the birthing question of our ecology of community: under what generic circumstances will hitherto separate groups come to see that the commonality of this task is important — as important or more important than the differences which distinguish and separate them?

I have elsewhere outlined three important dimensions of the quest: (a) the prerequisite self-governance which assures a safe home for differences; (b) the conducting of conversations in the mode of reciprocity, free from the manipulations of dominance and power; and (c) the actual creation of the material conditions of genuine partnership so that participants in the associated activity accurately perceive themselves to be equal shapers of a common future.[9] These activities, not usually described as religious activities, are far more important than isolated conversations of respect among ecumenical theologians to the creation of human planetary solidarity.

IV

In the meantime, while we are dying for our differences and until such time as differences do have a safe home, what are we to make of the notion of human and planetary solidarity? To see the joys and sufferings of other people and other species as related to and/or interdependent with our own, of course, remains a noble ideal. But this solidarity, it must be acknowledged, is an ideal, not a fact. This is not to deny that we are already highly interdependent or that we have many things in common. But these things in common are at most a necessary and not a sufficient condition for generating and sustaining human and planetary solidarity. Until those commonalities are perceived by all the relevant parties as of comparable importance as the differences, we will continue to live and to die for the differences.

Finally, one task of politics and of the imaginative arts is to help us see the joys and sufferings of all living things as related to ours. There is nothing or no one outside the pale. The love and reverence, or at least the civility, which could be expected to flow from such a vision precludes not only the extermination of any people or species but also the domination, neglect, or even caricaturing of any people or species. It is a fundamental religious principle that we all have business together. Or as Merton phrased it to Suzuki, we are "fellow citizens."[10] However unintelligible or bizarre or foreign or unarticulatable the expression, we will yet believe that somehow we are related or relatable to it. And it is this vision of ultimate relatability which rescues us, theologically speaking, from relativistic indifference; and which I take to be the only justification for continuing to speak in cautious tones about human nature, or about a Catholic Church, or about the existence of just one God.

Recalling in a positive though cautious tone this vision of a universal community might well cause confusion. Should we be more concerned with human solidarity than with human differences? My response is that for the most part human and planetary solidarity are best advanced by creating the aforementioned structures and conditions wherein (a) differences have their home and (b) nonmanipulative and reciprocal interaction is possible. In such conditions, unimpeded by theologies which discourage conversations of respect, and in response to the stimulus of artists and political visionaries, human solidarity will flow from the work and erotic play of primary communities in interaction. Within the context of democratic values, that is the only acceptable path.

Builders of community of the kind just described might well anchor themselves to a degree with the vision of or faith in ultimate relatability. But that faith is not such as to distinguish the believer, behaviorally speaking, from the nonbeliever. This chiaroscurist situation was well described by Emmanuel Monnier, the French personalist upon whom I cut my philosophical teeth at Boston University almost twenty-five years ago. "The course of Christian history," he wrote,

> is like that of those peaceful waters where we know indeed that they flow and whither, but where we cannot see, through gazing at one point, the direction in which, at this point, they are flowing. The landscapes are confused and values shrouded. Shadow alternates ironically with light, and immediate significance evades apprehension. The man of faith will never experience the total dereliction known to the philosopher of the absurd. But being so made as to create obscurity by the very audacity of his inquiry, he can escape neither creative anguish nor the combat in the night. Thus he becomes brother to all who, like him, are passionately involved in the search for the secret of man's being.[11]

NOTES

1. Raymond Williams, *Keywords* (New York: Oxford University Press, 1976), p. 66.

2. The term *ecology of community* is borrowed from my colleague Professor Donna Kerr at the University of Washington.

3. John Dewey, *Democracy and Education* (New York: Free Press, 1976), p. 86.

4. Rosemary Radford Ruether, *Women-Church* (New York: Harper & Row, 1986), p. 38.

5. There are excesses to be avoided, as Dewey noted, particularly those which threaten the existence of other communities and those which might yield a systematic or long-term isolation from other communities (Dewey, *Democracy and Education*, p. 99).

6. Cf. the observation of Henry Adams: "Everyone who has lived since the sixteenth century has felt deep distrust of everyone who lived before it," from *Mont-Saint-Michel and Chartres*, quoted in Morris Berman, *Coming to Our Senses* (New York: Simon & Schuster, 1989), p. 221.

7. The phrase *theological Rubicon* emerged in a 1986 conference of theologians at the Claremont Graduate School in California. For a description of the emergence of the concern, see John Hick and Paul F. Knitter, eds., *The Myth of Christian Uniqueness* (Maryknoll, N.Y.: Orbis Books, 1987). To gain a sense of the challenge of that concept, see Paul F. Knitter, "Hans Küng's Theological Rubicon," in *Toward a Universal Theology of Religion*, ed. Leonard Swidler (Maryknoll, N.Y.: Orbis Books, 1985), pp. 224–30.

8. My first exposure to thinking about religions in this manner was in a too-neglected book of Sterling Lamprecht's, *Our Religious Traditions* (Cambridge, Mass.: Harvard University Press, 1950). Lamprecht sees Judaism exploring the spiritual dimensions of the idea of covenant, Catholicism exploring the spiritual dimensions of community (or, as he phrases it on p. 37, the "corporate relationship with a funded wisdom accumulated in the experience of the saints through the generations"), and Protestantism, antithetically, exploring "the hazard of individual commitment" (p. 60).

9. See Patrick Hill, "The Search for Commonality in a Diverse World," *Frontiers of American Philosophy* 2: 6–11.

10. Thomas Merton, *Zen and the Birds of Appetite* (New York: New Directions Press, 1968), p. 138.

11. Emmanuel Monnier, *Studies in Personalist Sociology (La petit peur du XXe siècle)*, published as a single volume with *What Is Personalism? (Qu'est-ce que le personalisme?)* under the title *Be Not Afraid*, trans. Cynthia Rowland (New York: Sheed & Ward, n.d.), p. 84.

10
Knowing and Community
JÜRGEN MOLTMANN

I. THE PROBLEM OF LIKE AND UNLIKE

KNOWING AND COMMUNITY are mutually related to one another: in order to come together in community, we must know each other; and in order to know one another, we must come into contact with each other and enter into a relationship with one another. Community in personal as in political life most essentially depends on our being in a position to become aware of *the others*, to acknowledge them and to know them. Otherwise we only reflect ourselves in the others and accept them according to our image in order to subject them to our ideas. On the other side, our perceptions and our images of the other are always influenced by our social relationships to them and our public forms of community with them. One could also say: without knowledge no community and without community no knowledge.

If this rather general association is correct, then it follows that sociology and the theory of knowledge are so closely related to one another that laws in one field recur in the other field and changes in one field bring about changes in the other. I want to analyze this connection in this paper. My starting point is an assumption which came to me early on and which I have repeatedly mentioned.

Since Aristotle, the principle of knowledge has been: "Like is known only by like" (*Metaphysics* 2.4.100065). Since Aristotle, the principle of community has been: "Like seeks after like" (*Nicomachean Ethics* 8.1155a3). The principle of correspondence in the theory of knowledge and the homogeneity principle in the theory of society are identical.

But are they true? Do they serve the knowing of the other?

Do they lead to a living community with others? It certainly makes sense at the first glance that these principles, taken alone, result in only the opposite or nothing at all. If like is known only by like, then why should it be known at all? Is the like not fully indifferent to the like? If I know only the like or only what already corresponds to me, then I only know what I already know, and the fascination of knowing is lacking. The interest in knowing becomes paralyzed. "There is nothing new under the sun." Even the contrary thesis suggests itself here: "Like cannot be known by like, at all."

If socially like only aspired to be with like, wouldn't total desolation then enter into a society? The rich among themselves and the poor among themselves; the whites among themselves and the blacks among themselves; the men among themselves and the women among themselves; the healthy among themselves and the handicapped among themselves; each would stay with their like and none would know the others. This would be the totally segregated society of disconnected ghettoes and in each ghetto death through boredom.

Shouldn't one therefore attempt to begin from the opposite principles in order to come to the knowledge of the other and to community with the other: in the theory of knowledge, from the principle "Different is known only by different"; in the doctrine of society, from the principle "Community in diversity makes life interesting"? I call the first the analogy and homogeneity principle and the second the principle of difference and heterogeneity. I next want to present each of these principles in more detail. I will examine each of them according to the knowledge of other humans; of the other, nature; and of the totally other, God; by asking to which forms of community they lead. Finally, I will ask about the basis of knowledge of the humans, of nature, and of God in the elementary amazement about existence.

II. CORRESPONDENCE IN KNOWLEDGE LEADS TO COMMUNITY OF LIKE AND THOSE MADE LIKE

"Like is known only by like." If this principle of likeness is understood in a strict manner in the theory of knowledge, then something different can not be known at all. Then knowing is only a recognition of the already known and nothing other than the "eternal return of the same." Early Greek philosophy, therefore, immediately extended this principle to the similar: "Similar is known only by similar." Our knowing is based on analogy when we ask for the *tertium comparationis.* In areas of difference, the knowing one perceives the similar, that is, what corresponds to him or her, because only the other which finds a correspondence within the knowing ones is perceived by them. The macrocosmos outside corresponds to the microcosmos inside. All knowing of things in the outer world brings forth an echo in the inner world, and in this manner knowledge comes to exist. Today we would say: only when the receiver is tuned to the same frequency as the transmitter can the receiver hear the transmitter. Therefore Empedocles, from whom this principle of the theory of knowledge originated, says: "Sweet seized sweet and bitter rose to meet bitter, sour went to sour, hot quickly caught up hot. The fire sent forth, desiring to reach its like." For "with the earth (that is, within us) do we see earth, with water water, with air the divine air, but with fire consuming fire; with love we see love, strife with dead strife."[1]

The interest by which knowledge is directed here is the unification of the like in the human with the like in the cosmos. Like strives for like in order to unite with it. It is the power which creates the universe and holds it together, the power of eros which leads to the knowing of like through like.

Identity between the macro- and the microcosmos is what makes human knowing of the world possible, and knowing leads the humans to community with the world through correspondence of inside and outside. This ontological principle makes possible the unity through knowing, because in the ancient Greek world — as well as in the world of the Old Testament — knowing always created community. Knowing is deeply erotic: "Now Adam knew Eve . . ." (Gen. 4:1) and the result was their son Cain. But in what exists the power of eros? It lies in the attraction of the lovable (*eidos*) for the love (*eros*), of the excitement for the desire, and of the valuable for the appreciation. The power of eros is the power of knowing and of unification and must therefore be viewed as the basis of this theory of knowledge as well as this sociology.

I will now apply this principle to the knowing of other humans, of other things, and of the totally other God.

(a) If only like ones know one another, then I only know in other humans that which corresponds to me in my being. I do not perceive that which is different and alien about the other humans; I block it out. I only know that which is the same in both of us and only that can become the basis of community between us. "True friendship," says Aristotle, "exists on the basis of likeness" (*Nicomachean Ethics* 8.4). Friendship of like ones was the embodiment of the Greek doctrine of society. Although some heroes were called friends of the gods, one cannot actually speak of a friendship of the humans with the god-father Zeus. This is also the case between men and women, between the free and the slaves. On the basis of likeness, friendship operates in an exclusive manner. From like ones only closed societies arise. In them, the like ones mutually affirm their identity through the exclusion of the others and the repeated assurance of not being like the others. Even in our so-called open society, the like ones come together in exclusive circles. Not only is such behavior painful for the excluded *others;* it leads those who are *in* into a deadly boredom because they have already heard a hundred times all of the stories and jokes with which closed societies usually entertain themselves. The "eternal return of the same" is in fact not an image of eternity, but rather of the dying of the living.

The principle of correspondence does not lead to a gain in knowledge but rather to the constantly repeated self-verification of what is already known. The principle of likeness leads to caste and class societies and destroys the interest in the vivacity of life.

(b) When we apply this principle of knowledge to nature, then the consequence is ambivalent: in antiquity knowing meant *participation.* I know the nature outside by the nature inside of me in order to participate through my nature in the whole of nature and to be united with it. Reason was essentially perceptive reason, a thinking with the eyes (*theorein*), which see what is there. But modernity developed an understanding of the human as person and subject over against a nature which is made the object of human knowledge. Since Francis Bacon and René Descartes, knowing has meant domination: I want to know the nature outside in order to dominate it. I want to dominate it so that I can acquire it. I want to acquire it in order to do with my property what I want. This is thinking with the grasping hand.

The reason of modern, so-called scientific-technological civilization is no longer understood as a perceptive organ but as an instrument of power. The reason of the modern world which is influenced by natural science, according to Immanuel Kant, who philosophically rationalized Newton's world view, "only understands that which it produces according to its design. . . . It goes ahead with principles of its judgments according to steadfast laws and to press nature to answer its questions" (preface to the second edition of *The Critique of Pure Reason*). Human reason relates to nature like a judge who cross-examines the witnesses. According to Francis Bacon, experiments are the torture to which nature is subjected in order to answer human questions and to expose its secrets. But if this aggressive reason only understands of nature that which it *produces* on nature according to its own design, then the other and alien in nature remain eternally concealed from it. There can be no knowledge of the thing-in-itself, as Kant has made clear. But if this is correct, then humanity lives in the nature which has been manifested by the natural sciences as in a closet of mirrors: wherever one glances, one only sees the projections, the reflections, and the traces of the humans. Productive reason is only in a position to recognize its own products. It knows nothing of the thing's interior and of nature's own life. If "like is known only by like," then only the nature which is adapted, made like, and subjugated to this human reason is known by it. This however destroys nature's own life and alienates humans. Technopolis and the desert are left over. We have made the earth into the stonepit of our civilization and into its garbage dump.

(c) Applied to God, the principle of likeness leads either to the deification of the human or to the humanization of God. In antiquity, a deification of the human (*theosis*) was seen in every true knowledge of God, because we can only know the divine in us. For this reason, Goethe wrote:

> Were not the eye like the sun
> how could it look at the sun?
> Were not God's own power with us,
> how could the divine delight us?

Knowledge creates community and only the community of the like character makes such knowledge possible. Here again one needs to be aware that according to ancient understanding, knowledge changes the knowing one so that he or she corresponds to the known.

But is God then to be known at all by nondivine beings? Goethe gave the theological principle of equality an especially interesting turn: if God is only known by God, then the reverse is also true; no one is against God but God. It is not clear from whom Goethe has this powerful sentence or if his editor, F. W. Riemer, coined this statement and then presented it as old. Goethe placed this saying as motto above the fourth book of his autobiography, *Poetry and Truth* (*Dichtung und Wahrheit*), which he wrote in 1830. There he speaks of "demoniac" personalities which appear to stand beyond good and evil. He concludes: "Rarely or never do contemporaries experience themselves as alike, and they can not be conquered but through the universe itself with which they have begun to struggle; and from such remarks that strange but mighty saying may have arisen: no one against God but God himself." Eduard Spranger pursued this notion and found in Riemer's "Information about Goethe" Goethe's explanation: "A delightful saying of unlimited use. God always encounters himself; God in the human again in the human himself. . . ."[2] In the sense of Spinoza, whom Goethe honored, this sentence then reads: God is everything and in everything. If there is something contrary to the divine, then this contradiction against God also lies in God's self, because other than God's self there is no one who could fight against God. Even in the hardest *contra-Deum* (against God) still lies hidden *Deus ipse* (God's self). In itself, however, this sentence makes God's self the only conceivable atheist. If no one except God's self can be "against God" then human atheism is impossible. Or, alternatively, this sentence deifies all serious atheists who are "against God." As mighty as this sentence sounds and as fascinating as the possibilities of thinking are which it opens up, it can also be used for theological self-immunization. God is only known by God; no one can be against God except God. But that which makes itself invulnerable in theology, that we cannot be opposed to it, also really no longer concerns us.

Modern reason understands the process of knowledge in exactly the opposite way: through knowing the known is subjected and adapted to the knowing one because to know means to dominate. Applied to the divine above us, the principle of likeness therefore leads to understanding all knowledge of God as projection of human fantasy. All images and terms of the divine are only human products and express nothing about the divine itself. "You are like the spirit which you understand, not like me," says the "earth spirit" in Goethe's drama to Dr. Faust, who wants to conjure him. Therefore humans create their gods according to their images: masculine gods for the men and feminine gods for the women. The donkey would perhaps pray to donkeylike gods. The other, the alien and — as Karl Barth said — the "totally other" of the divine is in this manner unrecognizable so that it cannot even be thought of. The principle of likeness makes the reason of the modern world principally agnostic. It makes reason, as the modern critique of religion of Feuerbach proves, even narcissistic. Wherever the modern person turns, to other humans or to the other nature or to the totally other of the divine, he or she only sees, like the beautiful youth Narcissi, his or her own reflection everywhere. However, the enchanted self-love of the old Narcissi has in the meantime become lost to us, and for many it has already changed into the self-hate which strikes humans when they have closed themselves up and no longer can come out. A kind of claustrophobic self-pity has come into existence out of which only occasionally a "longing for the totally other" arises.[3]

As an example, let us take the great event which is at the beginning of the modern world because it has changed the world: the so-called discovery of America by Columbus, Cortes, and the conquistadors in 1492. As T. Todorov shows in his study *The Conquering of America: The Problem of the Other*,[4] America was never really "discovered" by the Europeans with its own character and differentness. The conquistadors saw nothing and "discovered" only what they were searching for, that is, gold and silver. The Indian empires were never known. They have never been understood, not even today. They were subjected, destroyed, and exploited and missionized and colonialized according to European designs. The other humans were adapted to the dominating ones as subjects. Also *Las Casas* and the Christian missionaries only understood that which they could make like themselves through conversion, as their diaries prove. The Spanish, the Portuguese, and the English Pilgrims did not know the differentness and the character of the Indians. Because they could only know and understand what was like them, they had to destroy the foreign cultures and make the other humans like themselves. The sad results were the colonial standard culture, the imperial standard religion, and the leveling standard language.

III. THE KNOWLEDGE OF THE OTHER LEADS TO COMMUNITY IN DIVERSITY

"Different is known only by different." This principle of the theory of knowledge also has its roots in the ancient Greek philosophy in a tradition which has, however, gained only limited influence in our culture. Euripides, whom Aristotle quotes, wrote: "The dry earth longs for rain; the high sky longs to precipitate down to the earth full of rain" (quoted in Aristotle, *Nicomachean Ethics* 8.2.1155b).

"Everything alive arises from conflict," said the mysterious Heraclitus. It was, however, only Anaxagoras who formulated principles of knowledge which are opposed to those of Empedocles. "Anaxagoras thinks that perception is by opposites, for like is not affected by like. . . . We know cold by warm, fresh by salt and sweet by bitter. . . . Every perception is accompanied by pain . . . for everything unlike produces pain by its contact."[5]

The last remark about the relationship of knowledge and pain is important. When our sensory organs encounter something like, something familiar, or something that already corresponds to us, we then feel affirmed and take comfort from this harmony. When our sensory organs encounter something different, alien, or new, pain arises. We feel the resistance of the alien. We feel the contradiction of the different. We notice the demand of the new. The pain indicates that we must change ourselves if we want to understand the alien, to perceive the different, and to comprehend the new. The pain indicates that we must open ourselves in order to receive the different, alien, and new. But by what means do we perceive it? We do not perceive it through its correspondence but rather through its contradiction. One first knows the things through their opposition to what they are not. With the contrary in us, we know the different. Not through consonance but rather through dissonance do we become awake to the new. According to the imagery of Anaxagoras, the darker it is in us, the more we experience the brightness of the light. The colder we are, the stronger we experience the warmth of a fire. Among blacks we notice that we are white; among whites that we are black. In a figurative sense, "every being can be revealed only in its opposite. Love only in hatred, unity only in conflict," as the young Schelling dialectically formulated it.[6] Expressed somewhat less dramatically, only when we are far away do we understand what home means. Only in the face of death do we feel the uniqueness of life. Only in conflict do we come to appreciate peace. In the like, we do not even notice the like. It is self-evident. It is so close to us that we can not even know it. Only in the distance and even more in the difference and then finally in the contradiction do we perceive the different and come to appreciate it.

The directing interest here is again unification. The goal, however, is not a unity in uniformity, but rather a unity in diversity. Differences can complement one another and long for mutual completion, as the earth for rain and the rain for the earth. Differences can also fight with one another and produce new life out of their fight. Antagonisms need not always be deadly. They can also make alive and encourage life. By "fight" (*agon*) Heraclitus did not mean war, but rather the contest and the game as "father of all things." These are polarities which continually separate and unite themselves; they separate themselves in order to unite; they unite in order to separate, and in this way advance the process of life. The power of the unification of the differences and the power of the separation of the united here also is eros, but in a deeper understanding than previously mentioned. It is the dynamic dialectics of love (Hegel), which creates unity in separation and separation in unity because it is the unity of separation and unity itself.

I will now apply these dialectical principles to the knowing of other humans, other things, and the totally other God.

(a) If unlikes know each other then the interest in the differentness of the other must be greater than in the likeness of the other. I do not focus on what is like me in the other but rather on what is different, and I attempt to understand it. I understand it only in that I alter myself and adjust myself to the different. In my knowledge of the other, I subject myself to the pain and joys of my own change, not in order to adapt myself to the different but in order to take the perspective of the different. There is no real understanding of the other without such empathy. I enter into a process of reciprocal change with the other. All processes of learning contain these pains of change and the joys of new insights. In Greek, the words *mathein* ("to learn") and *pathein* ("to suffer") belong together in many sayings. Out of the understanding empathy arises a connecting sympathy when the empathy leads to mutual understanding. It forms community in diversity and diversity in community. The basic principle of a healthy society is the acknowledgment of others in their differentness. Societies which develop on the basis of this principle are not closed societies, nor are they uniform societies; rather, they are open societies. They can live not only with various and different people but rather, as Karl Popper demanded, also with their enemies because they can even make the hostility of their enemies fruitful. How is this possible? Must the enemies of a society be told: "Love it or leave it"? No. Just like love of the friend normally is the basis of the society of like ones, the basis of the society of different ones is, in serious situations, love of the enemy. To love one's enemies means to take responsibility not only for oneself and one's own people but also for one's enemies. We then no longer only ask, How can we protect ourselves against the possible enemy? but rather, How can we take away the hostility from enemies so that we can survive together with them? In this sense love of the enemy is the basis for a common life in conflicts.

(b) If we apply this dialectical principle of knowledge to nature, we then replace analytical isolating thinking, and its objectivization of nature, with communicative thinking which respects nature in its own character and lets it be in its relation to the human. This means, first of all, to perceive natural beings in their wholeness and in their life worlds and no longer to isolate and split them. Second, this means to acknowledge them in their relative subjectivity and no longer to degrade them as objects. The interest by which knowledge is directed is no longer domination and control, but rather communication. Holistic thinking again leads humans into the web of the life community in the greater

organism of this earth, out of which they have arisen to be domi-
nators and owners of nature by virtue of science and technology.
Ending this self-isolation does not mean a romantic return to
paradise-like natural states and "Mother Earth," but rather a new
integration of human culture with nature, balancing the various
life interests. This includes on the part of humans a reintegration
of the differentiating and dominating intellect into the receiving
and participating reason, but it goes beyond this.

The new participating reason is also always an interested reason. It does not observe and dominate things and other living beings in their achieved reality but rather understands their reality
together with their possibilities in order to prevent destructive possibilities and to encourage possibilities which serve life. Interested
thinking asks not only how things are but also what can become
of them. With the condition of things it also knows their future.
It understands all things in their time and living beings in their
processes.

This, on the other hand, presupposes an understanding of objects of nature as systems open to the future, whose past is defined,
whose future is partly undetermined, and whose present consists
in the anticipation of their possibilities. If from the atom to humans all beings are open systems as I. Prigogine and others correctly say, then there are, strictly speaking, no *objects* in nature
but rather only subjects with varying degrees of complexity. Human knowledge of natural things is therefore nothing other than
communication between open systems of various degrees of complexity. It is therefore a process of knowledge between subject and
subject. Between different subjects, however, the question is about
community in acknowledgment of diversity; power and control
from one side would only destroy the variety of the living and their
life relationships.

(c) Applied to God, dialectical thinking leads to the acknowledgment of diversity in community. "God is known only by God,"
says the likeness principle. But it is doubtful if God looks at God
as *God* or if God only appears as God to humans. Dialectical thinking says that God appears as God in the realm of what is different
from God, that is, in the realm of humans; dialectical thinking
says that for humans God is totally other. Only when humans understand themselves simply as humans and no longer as gods are

they in a position to perceive God's totally other character. Only if we once again return to being completely human and cease to be unhappy supermen and superwomen and pathetic minigods do we allow God to be God, as Luther said. One can go a step further and say: only when we humans become completely godless, in the sense that we give up all self-deification or presumed likeness to God, can we know the totally other reality of the true God.

"To know God means to suffer God" is an old Greek saying based on experience. The God-experiences of Abraham, Isaac, and Jacob, the God-experiences of Moses and Jesus confirm this. Humans perceive the totally other reality of God only in pain. These are, according to the Christian experience, the pains of dying from God and the joys of being born anew from God. Only through total change of ourselves do we perceive the totally other reality of God. The theological climax of this type of God-knowledge came through the "theology of the cross," according to which God is hidden under the cross and suffering; and therefore, the real misery of humans which appears God-forsaken is the location at which God encounters us. "In the moments of God's deepest revelation there was always some suffering: the cry of the oppressed in Egypt, the cry of Jesus on the cross, the birth pains of the entire creation which awaits its liberation."[7] If God is revealed in his opposite, he can be known by the godless and God-forsaken ones, and this very knowledge brings them into correspondence with God and, as 1 John 3:2 says, even into the hope of God's likeness.[8]

Is this dialectical knowing identical with that medieval principle of analogical knowing according to which there is, with all the similarity between creature and Creator, a still greater dissimilarity between them? "Because it is impossible to perceive such a similarity between Creator and creature that the greater dissimilarity between them would not have to be perceived."[9]

This dissimilarity within all similarity differentiates the Creator from the creature in an ideal manner. But for us there is the contradiction of the sinner against God and God's merciful revelation to the godless. The knowledge of God for the truly godless ones can only come through their acceptance of the crucified Christ: "Immanuel — God with us — with us godless ones!"[10] On the basis of this God-knowledge it is possible to speak again of the relationship of the human creature to the Creator. God's contradiction against our contradiction creates correspondences and similarities with ever greater ontological dissimilarity.

IV. THE ORIGIN OF KNOWING IN AMAZEMENT

In the concrete process of knowing, we always combine the moments of correspondence and the moments of contradiction. If there was nothing alike, then there would also be nothing in common and, therefore, also no possibility of knowing. If there was nothing different, then there would also be no need to know. In concrete knowing, we need the affirmation through the correspondence and the pain through the contradiction. Knowing is remembering and expecting; remembering the known and expecting the new is recognizing and knowing anew.

But where does the root of knowing lie? There are of course as many interests which direct knowing as there are human wishes. But with them only the subjective factors are named which take hold of an ability to know which is already there and must be presupposed. The root for knowing itself is not only subjective, but rather at the same time also objective. It lies in the elementary form of the encounter of the awaking senses of humans with the impressions of the world. The Greek philosophers have therefore named the deepest reason of knowing *amazement*. In amazement, the senses open themselves for the immediate impressions of the world. In amazement the perceived things penetrate fresh and unfiltered into human sensory organs. They impress themselves on humans. They impress us and we are impressed. In amazement, the things are perceived for *the first time*. The amazed child does not yet possess any ideas with which he or she can grasp impressions, nor any terms with which he or she can limit them. Only on the second and third time does the child remember and acquire a repeatable attitude toward the intruding impressions. By the twentieth time, this perception is then already familiar and one reacts with intellect and will as one has learned it. It no longer amazes one. One is no longer surprised. One has become adjusted to it, as we say. For this reason, we adults attribute the amazement to children's eyes that perceive and experience the world for the first time.

However, on the whole, a small bit of amazement remains in the perceptions of adults. Because in the temporal reality of life nothing repeats itself in the strict sense, but rather every moment is unique; only the amazement in us is capable of capturing the unique moments. Those who can no longer be amazed, those who have become accustomed to everything, those who only routinely perceive and react miss reality. Each chance is unique. This belongs to its character. The same chance does not occur twice. There is no "second chance," because time is irreversible. "No one steps into the same river twice" (Heraclit). Those people who have preserved their original capacity for amazement have a feel for the uniqueness of the moment. They perceive the uniqueness of the moment with that openness with which they grasped the newness of things.

In amazement, we do not yet grasp how things look but we do grasp that they are there. We perceive with admiration that they are there. We understand in an elementary manner the miracle of existence itself. We are often also amazed *that* we ourselves are there although we do not know why or for what reason we are there. Those who are amazed by this also experience that they are really there and do not represent an illusion. That means that through amazement we grasp the existence of the world and our own existence. The what and the how are comprehended later. But one never comprehends simple existence. It remains amazing.

Isn't it important to continually trace our knowing, the interests directing our knowledge, the ideas which we build from experiences, and the terms with which we order our ideas back to the elementary amazement about existence itself? Otherwise it could happen that we only see what we want to see because we search for it and go through life almost blind. It could otherwise be that we no longer know other humans because we have pinned them down through our prejudices and only want to have these prejudices confirmed. It could be that we mistake the products of our religious fantasy for God and notice nothing of the living God. The reality is always more surprising than we are able to imagine.

"Terms create idols, only amazement grasps something," said the clever Gregor of Nyssa (PG 44.377b). People whom we respect in their individuality remain amazing for us, and our amazement opens the freedom for new possibilities of the future of our community with them. The miracles of nature also remain amazing for us when we pause in our work and submerge ourselves in the sight of a flower or a tree or a sunset. To me, however, the most amazing appears to be the source of the existence of all things. Why is there anything at all rather than nothing at all? The one whom we call "God" escapes our imaginations, but is however closer to us than we are to ourselves. Amazement is the inexhaustible source of our community with one another, with nature, with God. Amazement is the beginning of each new experience and the source of our expectant creativity.

NOTES

1. W. Capelle, *Die Vorsokratiker* (Berlin, 1958), pp. 217f., 236.

2. Eduard Spranger has gone into this more precisely in "Nemo contra Deum nisi Deus ipse" (1949) in *Philosophie und Psychologie der Religion* (Tübingen, 1974), pp. 315ff. See also C. Schmitt, *Politische Theologie* 2 (Berlin, 1970), pp. 116, 123ff.; and Jürgen Moltmann, *Der gekreuzigte Gott* (Munich, 1972), pp. 145f.

3. Max Horkheimer, *Die Sehnsucht nach dem ganz anderen* (Hamburg, 1970), pp. 56ff.

4. T. Todorov, *Die Eroberung Amerikas: Das Problem des Anderen* (Frankfurt, 1985).

5. Theophrastus, *De sensibus* 27ff., quoted in G. M. Straton, *Theophrast and the Greek Physiological Psychology before Aristotle* (New York, 1917), pp. 90ff.

6. F. W. J. Schelling, *Über das Wesen menschlicher Freiheit* (1809; Reclam no. 8913–15, 89).

7. I. Sobrino, "Theologisches Erkennen in der europaischen und der lateinamerikanischen Theologie," in *Befreiende Theologie*, ed. Karl Rahner (Stuttgart, 1977), p. 138.

8. Moltmann, *Der gekreuzigte Gott*, p. 33.

9. Fourth Lateran Council 1215, in H. Denzinger, *Enchiridion Symbolorum* (Freiburg, 1947), no. 202. Cf. E. Przywara, *Religionsphilosophie katholischer Theologie* (Munich, 1926).

10. Karl Barth, *Kirchliche Dogmatik* 1.1 (Zurich, 1932, 1952), sec. 3, pp. 47ff.

11

The Apocalypse of Community

CATHERINE KELLER

THE TITLE OF THIS ESSAY entertains an ambiguous proposition. It suggests threat and revelation; finally it recommends disclosure, the originating etymology of *apokalypsis*. The present essay is composed for the particular communicative purposes of a colloquium series and an oral discussion. It begins, and only begins, to unfold an implication of the apocalyptic myth for the overused but under-realized notion of *community*. I hope it comes to fruition in the larger work in which I am engaging the edges of eschatology. It prepares ground for encounter with the literature of community and communitarianism, but hardly begins to construct. Foundations seem to be lacking, in fact and of necessity. To claim that "community is in apocalypse" signals significatory as well as social distress. The floundering and perhaps the foundering of the very concept of *community* belongs to the signs of the times which a feminist counterapocalyptic cannot ignore.

In the premodern world various levels of community, centered in the extended family, tribal, and village structures, could be taken for granted. But urbanization and empire building were persistently cracking and eroding kinship networks, fissuring communities along the lines of class and caste and uprooting human community from its bed in the earth. Whole classes of marginalized slaves and wanderers emerged, most notably the *hapiru*, who formed the nation of Israel around the pathos of return of "the People" to "the Land." Thus it is no accident that it was this people, after too much exile and too little return, who finally gave birth to the genre of apocalypse, with its desperate yearning for a new heaven and earth. Its profoundly alienated hope comes out

177

of the frustrated yearnings of aliens for a cosmologically embedded community. It is not surprising that such far-fetched hope was necessary to retain faith in an ever unfulfilled Promise; and that the apocalyptic hope has had such resonance among the marginalized of subsequent Western history.

That this hope was forged in a patrilineal and patricentric society, however, and that the promise was to patriarchs from a deity forged in their image, is also not surprising, as the entire late neolithic–early bronze age process of urbanization, class stratification, and imperial conquest is coextensive with the codification of patriarchal laws for women's sexual and economic subordination.[1] Hebrew prophetic discourse is one long assault on the class and ethnic injustices of a patriarchal society. Yet it rarely even glimpses injustice against women as such. The Hebrews did not invent patriarchy, but they made it monolithic. Biblical eschatology shaped a vision of a single history controlled by a celibate male deity, who punishes and privileges a single community as the means to a single end.

Under the auspices of a search for identity inspired by a single One, the ingrained tendency of community to suppress or to exclude difference gained the new integrity of an elect. The biblical sense of oneness which is built on separation (*kadosh*) from the other and then, in strength, on suppression of the other, has profoundly shaped our sense of what community can mean. Community gradually collapsed into unity.

The apocalypticism of the early Christian movement has a paradoxical relation to this singular oneness. The Christian vision does in a certain sense break the monolith into trinitarian internal community. Yet it does so by the begetting of a celibate male Son, who must then return again, as despite the anti-Judaic arguments that the Messiah had finally come, the messianic age showed no worldly signs of having set in. The church as the new community of the elect was to hold out for the brief interim before the end. As in the Jewish apocalyptic communities, high expectancy of a near end gives solace and strength under intolerable pressure and, then as now, creates community. The alluring Pauline vision of the Body of Christ, whose intertwined members exhibit so promisingly the mutually participatory character of selves in community, is framed by the sharpness of its outer boundaries. That is, the fluid reciprocity of selves within the body seems to depend upon the absolutism with which the division between outsider and insider is drawn. When, three centuries later, Christianity offers itself as the spiritual infrastructure of the empire, this division loses all innocence. And whereas the apocalypticism of the early Christian community allowed for some significant experimentation in gender and class egalitarianism within the community, the ascetic and imperial church closed such eschatological loopholes.[2]

In other words, the Christian community, as it congealed into the unity of a church universal, came to accept difference only on the terms of conversion for outsiders and stratification for insiders. Anyone failing to meet these terms met with temporal punishment and eternal damnation.

Apocalypse as religious genre has in a sense compensated for the systemic destruction of organic communities characteristic of the patriarchal social experiment. It has also internalized and spiritualized the warrior impulse to conquer, to dominate, to win absolutely and live in immortal, jewel-encrusted splendor. Because Christianity happened to become the religion of empire in the West, these aspects of the apocalyptic fantasy, especially as repressed within the mainline church, themselves have then contributed to the systemic destruction. It seems to me then not an accident that it is specifically Christian civilization, with its secular transformations into individualism and collectivism, that has developed the technological means to literalize the apocalyptic doom portrayed in the final book of its Book of Books — precisely by way of a progressivist optimism (capitalist or revolutionary) which intended by those very means to bring about the new heaven and earth.

A feminist perspective discloses not only the patriarchy of apocalypse, but the apocalypse of patriarchy. We are not in a postpatriarchal situation. Yet there is at least unprecedented awareness of and resistance to the unacceptable violence against women built into the structures of our subjugation. There is as well an evolving understanding of how men suffer at the hands of their own role, which is to war against each other. That is, a successful patriarchal male is one who has his women under control and is thereby empowered to compete for dominance over other males.

That a women's movement has so stubbornly persisted has

to do with at least three factors. First, we are struggling for a future, one which we neither expect nor need to have wholly realized in our lifetimes. This is the eschatological factor. Patriarchal powers, on the other hand, tend to fixate on the past and its enfranchisement as present. As earlier apocalyptic movements demonstrate, presence energized by futurity has an extraordinary power to resist annihilation by these powers. Yet apocalyptic futurism and the secular utopias it spawned were generally no less patriarchal.[3] Feminist futures therefore firmly planted themselves in the present. Second, we enjoy community already, however unstable and fragmented; we take pleasure in our friendships with other women and with those men who in brave and quirky ways come through as allies. We are as white feminists suffering and fumbling our way through to respect for the stubborn differences between groups, classes, and races of women as well. We sometimes actually relish difference without mere endless deferring. We have some fun along the way, no matter what. This is the factor of connection-in-difference. Third, this future-creating communing, or community-creating future, takes place on the surface of the earth. This is the ecofeminist factor. We seek a grounded, ecohistorical presence to the future. Feminist theory has with some success been working itself out of the polarizations of nature versus history, which in religion takes the form of goddess naturalism versus historical messianism, and ecological-cultural versus structural and poststructuralist analysis. This dialectic may yield sane thoughts about how to be intersubjectively activated human animals on an imperilled planet. If there is to be a new heaven and earth, it can only take place as a renewal of this sky, ground, water.[4]

Because of the radical transformation of community required for such a renewal — a kind of self-consciousness that could only perhaps emerge pending apocalypse — it will be new indeed. The more ecocentric and egalitarian communities of other cultures and other epochs could take much for granted that can never be taken for granted again. And this in itself is not bad: the taken-for-grantedness of an endless natural world and of human clan and community grounds itself historically in the subjugation of women as wife-mothers who can be "taken"— as grants from neighboring tribes, fathers, slave traders, priests, gods, or God.

This taken-as-and-for-grantedness helps to explain why Western conceptions of freedom so often focus on freedom *from* — from not only pharaoh and the whore of Babylon, but from community, from clan, from family, from mother, indeed from all that could be taken for granted.

Of course such breakaway impulses cannot be lumped simply together, any more than "communities" can be. Thus Jesus' antifamily sentiment pits the eschatological community of the future against the communities of origin, especially of kin. By contrast, modern conservative individualism, like ancient patriarchy, builds itself on strong bonds of family loyalty. One of the great ironies of the religious right's apocalypticism is its attempt to build its "profamily" ideology on its christocentric biblicism. (Note the merger of profamily with capitalist-individualist rhetoric.) Given the massive erosion of any communal systems, the appeal of the "return to family" ideology is understandable. But whatever can be said of Jesus, he was no family man. The away-from impulse may not be antirelational, in a situation in which the given community, as taken-for-granted, functions to define the limits of acceptable relationship.

The image of the lone prophet, the pilgrim, the knight of the grail, the alienated existentialist, the new age spiritual journeyer — these are patterns of individualization that yield possibilities inhibited by the communities of origin. Yet they are instances of the archetype of the hero. The messiah figure of Revelation represents the goriest recrudescence in the Bible to the warrior hero. Jungians accurately analyze the hero warrior myth as the paradigm of masculine ego development (which women must also undertake if they wish to individuate). They inaccurately, however, make massive cultural patterns into eternal archetypes. Yet the critique of oppressive community, the impulse to liberate oneself and even one's people from the community of origin or the status quo, is readily drawn to the andromorphic hero myth. Communities of exclusion inspire individualism, often infusing it with the feeling of liberation. The hero then wanders into anomic individualism or forms a new patriarchy. That is, it is extremely difficult under the dysrelational circumstances of cumulative alienation to generate alternatives to totalistic community and irresponsible privacy.

The movement beyond the hero myth of patriarchy will then move us away from the romantic ethos of the mere away-from, or from the mere "post" of postmodernism, the mere negation of the negative, as matricide, patricide, liberation, or alienation. Otherwise our white middle class, feminist or not, will continue to fall prey to the cancerous individualism which is now, in the nineties, perhaps the greatest threat to this taken-for-granted planet and its taken-for-granted populations. Breaking away from alienated community justifies itself only in the creation of communities of shared freedom.

Futurity, difference, and earthiness: let these stand as criteria of what we may call a positive apocalypse — that is, a dis-closure of community. Community reveals itself as a force of resistance to all closure, to all coerced unities and forced ends. And it remains a hope, never a given. This then is the inverse sense in which community is in apocalypse.

Note that futurity as a value which implies and is implied by communities of resistance came into the human story as a contribution of the same prophetic eschatological justice tradition which under extremity gives birth to apocalypticism. But through the biblical secularization of nature, generated by the fierce sense of the one God, who could not be mixed up with the plural forces of nature, and the alienations of seminomadism and exile, community could gradually be dislodged from the land, until it reached its peaks of ascetic Christian otherworldliness. Thus Christian futurism has sadly intensified rather than healed the alienation from land, thus indirectly justifying the ecological indifference which has led us to the prospect of a truly unearthly future. And at the same time the apocalyptic tradition exaggerated the dualism of good and evil, of us and them, into the very paradigm for the singularity of community as the tiny group of the elect.

Community in the singular, the singularity of one voice, one set of beliefs, one nation under one God, one woman under one man, one race over others, even one feminism for all women, fails before the demands of pluralism. The revelation of the plurality of truth claims has taken on new urgency and new excitement at the end of modernity. The disclosure of community means exposure of the systemic unifiers which bond us over and against difference.

This is where much contemporary intellectual generativity is to be found, here in the struggle to articulate theories adequate to hear the others and yet to resist mere relativism, that is, a pluralism of indifference which cannot adjudicate the claims of truth and of injustice made by those very others. Other-hearing means first absolving myself of the hope of achieving an absolute unity of truth which would posit homogeneity as the basis for a community of discourse. Homogeneity makes community collapse into unity.

But this direction of reasoning might seem to cut against any community beyond that of special interest groups or organic affinity. The hope of community, when blown beyond its appropriate boundaries, becomes a form of imperialism. Such limitation on our projection of community is important for those of us operating out of positions of relative world privilege, for the extension of our communities into universality implies the universal extension of our privilege. Rather than declaring the universality of community, I can work to transform myself-in-community and my communities themselves, by taking responsibility for the ways in which I participate in and benefit from my community's oppression of more vulnerable ones.

This may involve first of all recognizing that while I feel consciously few bonds of identification with some set of "middle-class white North American persons," the individualism which allows me to dislodge myself from the instances of this community that have supported me is itself part of the problem of the white middle class. It is the very mechanism which enables us to understand ourselves as liberal exceptions who have transcended the exclusivist homogenizing tendencies of our communities of origin and therefore need not take responsibility for changing them. It also allows me to overlook the abysms of difference making up the boundaries between my communities and other, often more crushingly oppressed, communities. Friendship, warmth, pain, music, communication may cross these boundaries. But my main task remains, not the creation of some common ground between myself and the other community, but rather the transformation of the systemic unifiers of my own, to which those boundary crossings inspire.

At the same time, I don't see how to relinquish all hope for community between communities. Perhaps it comes down to this: I am not going to be long motivated to expose myself and my group to the pain of critique by the other unless I can entertain the hope of community with that other. Otherwise the motivation remains guilt, duty, and the appropriation of self-transforming resources, and the stale political correctitude of white middle-class "progressives." I do not need community now, with those who do not want it with me, but who nonetheless call me to accountability. But I do need the reciprocity of relationship in which accountability can happen; and when this begins to happen, then what is happening but the communication which makes community possible? I won't keep struggling to change if I cannot even *imagine* some massively, globally, finally inclusive sort of community. This hope does not imply that such community between communities will happen. It is a utopian hope, not a utopian faith. But I don't think we can ethically or psychologically afford to squelch that hope.

A certain internal resistance—whether from the other who is already among us, or the other who confronts us from without but whose challenge resonates within—creates the very opening in which its voice can be heard. And just in that prefigural way I do and must experience the hope of community with the other communities. These very others encounter me as more than individual, as the embodiment of another world, if these are others with whom I can never identify or unify but with whom I seek to be in political solidarity. Therefore these cross-communal encounters confront me already as a social being, already accountable for my "communities," such as they are.

In fact, community rarely appears as more than an evanescent dream, once it has terminally dislodged itself from some form of organic village commune. Its durability, even apart from premodern world orders, may have the character of a cumulative history claimed in acts of solidarity. But, as I suggested above, its liveliness at this point seems to take on more the aspect of a hope than of a historical fait accompli. Like all hope, however, it is not a hope that could be sustained unless it were already prefiguring its own object. That prefiguration seems not to occur apart from action, even organization. But of course organization does not guarantee it. It is just as likely to threaten as to guard the open-ended spontaneity which makes community worth hoping for. Only such open spaces within a community allow for real difference, which prevents relationships from collapsing in upon themselves, into unity.

Interrelationship is a fact which transcends the definitions and the boundaries of any particular community. Communities are networks in which that interdependence is perceived, intended, and enhanced. At the heart of the present apocalypse is the disclosure of our irrevocable ecological interdependence. Perhaps instead of the aim at universal community, which easily merges into some "new world order" controlled by the military and economic powers, our communities of communities will find their coherence outside of anthropocentrism. Perhaps it will rest in the fragile integrity of the earth. Perhaps the shared ecological circumstances of all earth beings can provide the encompassing breadth of interconnection from which no single community may abstract itself.

Let us return to the notion of a positive, or open, apocalypse. It may honor the real possibilities of community, and of community between communities, as these possibilities continue to disclose themselves. As for instance in Gloria Naylor's *The Women of Brewster Place*, which presents no naive idealization of African-American urban life, hope is always hope for community.[5] It brings with it bitter disappointments. But no horrifying pattern of oppression and despair serves as a terminal excuse to give up hope.

Community, like and with women, the earth, and the future, is no longer to be taken for granted. But let me address this from within the community of academic discourse in which this discussion is taking place. Two currents of late modern thinking seem to me to move toward a new consciousness of community. The first is the idea of the intrinsically relational self. The second is the interpretation of theory as emerging from and accountable to the praxis of communities.

The idea that the self is in a fundamental sense constituted by its relations is not an ancient idea. Though premodern thinkers certainly argued for the political character of the human animal, or for the necessity of the church for salvation, the internalization of community as the infrastructure of personality was only glimpsed as a theory. That is, the community of interest to premodern thinkers was that of the human soul with God or the One, and human and natural community was mediated through participation in universals. Selves were partitioned into faculties, but not analyzed as interpersonal activities. They could thence stride boldly into the age of the modern individual, as true "man of substance" touting his autonomous ego and breaking away from the bonds of community. Interestingly, the main predecessor for the relational self is found in the trinitarian analysis of God, a revelation felt as essential to Christian faith yet never applied to Christians.

Only by way of the modern apocalypse Nietzsche called "the death of God" did this structure of essential relatedness, in which the personal is the interpersonal, begin to come down to earth, into the construction of human psychology and even philosophical cosmology. Hegel and Marx develop radically communitarian accounts of human nature. Buber and the phenomenologists develop a later, existential strand of the discourse of intersubjectivity. And certain Anglo-American thinkers have played an impressive role in this declaration of the social nature of the self, notably Royce, James, Mead, Sullivan, and Whitehead.

But one can view the development of an ontology of relational being with ambivalence. It is as though once kinship and land-based communities were being irreversibly disrupted by the industrial revolution and the economics of individualism and of centralization, community was lifted into the self — precisely *as* social self — into a sphere more private than even the Victorian household. With the metaphysics of the relational self, community itself is preserved, even as it is being socially annihilated, by an act of intellectual transcendence. The community being smashed by external forces could now be enjoyed within.

Yet at the same time these schemes imply that the impoverishment of community directly impoverishes the self, which is dependent for its content upon its world. Josiah Royce, for instance, in whom Hegelianism intersects with American pragmatism and Bergsonian vitalism and becomes a key source for Marcel's existentialism, is an interesting case. He concludes Volume 1 of *The Problem of Christianity* by contextualizing his discussion as taking place early in a century which he predicted would undergo unfathomably accelerated rates of change, and in which "henceforth commerce and industry will tend to take the place in . . . minds which religious institutions once occupied." His core imperative is therefore not meant to address a timeless human situation, though it speaks to anyone who expects to find community ready-made: "The principle of principles in all Christian morals remains this:

—'Since you cannot find the universal and beloved community,—create it.'"[6]

Of course to us the language of universal community may ring imperial. The imperative seems to address the lone and empowered individual rather than the socially embedded self. And Royce's ultimate value of *loyalty* resounds with a hearty martial manly spirit, though it must be understood as a critique of Christian passivity, of waiting for the otherworldly kingdom rather than creating the beloved community now. My appreciation of this text is not strictly a case of my white middle class individualistic proclivities, I suspect, since Martin Luther King borrowed from Royce, via the Boston personalists, this idea of the beloved community.

These ideas, even at their most helpful, nonetheless remain ideas, embedded in systems which seem to lack any sense of accountability for their effects upon their communities. I want, rather, to walk a path so many women have trodden, one preferring the present crumbling tissue of relations as the way from past to future, one willing to eschew the drama of ancient or future absolutes in favor of what is emerging as possible among us, on the earth, here and now. Such imagination, born of the internalization of relations, does find a certain theoretical illumination in the philosophies of relational selfhood.

Yet this delicate tissue path can neither begin nor acquiesce in theory. It knows that even the most wonderfully relational of these manmade ontologies does a certain violence to the tissue, precisely because of the failure of all such post-Enlightenment liberal thought to take seriously its own life tissue, that is, the context, the community, the body in which the thoughts get thought. Therefore they naturally lack a structural account of the ways in which precisely by means of the web of relations, relations of injustice find their victims so vulnerable. Precisely through the interdependence of life do cycles of dominance by those who deny their own dependencies tie us all up into the closed loops of the present age. This is not to dismiss the disclosive power of such ontology; rather, it is to say that in and of itself, it does not have the power to expose the beasts of the present apocalypse. The alternative ontology may be needed, especially in the form of an earth-disclosing cosmology, as part of the strategic opposition to the sort of ontology implied in Margaret Thatcher's statement that "there is no such thing as community." Without an understanding that pluralism and reciprocal transformation belong to relatedness, and that relatedness is the matrix in which we come to be, the creation of communities remains an accident, an option. But the strategy is not generated out of ontology.

The real hope for theory lies in the interruption of theory by practice. If I nurture a certain millennialist interest in the accumulation of the markedly nonapocalyptic theories of communal selfhood, I find even greater significance in the striking proliferation over the past hundred or so years of social movements aiming at the creation of just, earthly community. Liberation and feminist theologies do not come raw to and from their praxis. Praxis is thoroughly interpretive; indeed, the liberation movements are directly, through prophetic texts, and indirectly, through revolutionary ideology, shaped for better or for worse by traditions of an apocalyptic interpretation of history. What is at stake is a new sense of accountability to one's community for the effects of one's interpretive action. Theory has not before on this scale taken accountability for particular historical situations. Philosophical theory in the West has held itself accountable only to something called *the truth;* theology has held itself accountable at best to the establishment church. What Foucault calls "the insurrection of subjugated knowledges" is interrupting — at least at the level of theory — the drive to power/knowledge of our "disciplines."[7] The subversive ideas disseminated in these fields can be neatly pruned or weeded out, unless the boundaries of the fields themselves and the techniques of their tending are persistently questioned. This seems more likely to happen where the pluralistic-interdisciplinary traditions of relational anthropology exercise direct influence — as in this Boston University colloquium, as in my graduate school experience at the Center for Process Studies, as in some programs in my present context, as in almost any women's studies context. Indeed I find this to be most promising where theological education, with its unavoidable links to the ecumenical churches, happens in cooperation with the university. The insurrection and exploration of hitherto marginalized communities of discourse has begun to stabilize a pattern of interruptions and openings within academic communities. These disunifying incursions of praxis into the heart of theory have not (yet?) been thoroughly coopted and do hold open realistic grounds for hopeful action.

Here, at the end of the millennium which is the millennium of the university, disillusionment may liberate, but alienation is self-indulgence. To wallow in disappointment remains an option when survival is not at stake — or not a value. Some space has been and is being claimed in which criteria of community, earth, and future can confront the academy and its worlds. This should be enough to start with. We need no grandiose and heroic apocalypses, no sudden conversions, and certainly no definitive conclusions. Relations of difference seek time/spaces for unfolding, not end-times for homogenizing.

Interrelatedness is a fact which theory may rightly ontologize. Community is not. Community is a cherished, chosen expanse of interrelation, in which relation itself is examined, maximized, nurtured, stretched; in which "loyalty" toward "the common good" is pursued; in which interrelationship becomes praxis. If the community turns in on itself, against the world, it will lose the art of difference even among its members; conversely, if it arranges its own members in hierarchy (beginning usually with the subjugation of women), it corrodes the intimate connection to connection itself. And if it happens to have the power to dominate the excluded others from the outside, of whom women may be the first instance in early history, it becomes a force for the conversion of community into imperial unity. This all went on. By and large only the communities with the martial disciplines and the inner hierarchies of empire survived to tell the stories of their lost paradise. The fast-forward story of the paradise to come, requiring either death or the apocalypse, held open an imaginal space, a utopic challenge, though it soaked the space with blood. "Communities of resistance and solidarity"[8] persist in generating hope from that space, and recreating the possibility of community.

Disclosure is always at once ontological and hermeneutical, that is, disruptive of a closure and revealing of a possibility. It requires only those abstractions which might be needed to keep our minds loyal to the project. Mostly it needs simple things for the effort, always again, to create just community for the future and of the earth: simple gifts like some place; time; love; communication; solidarity; difference; organization; ecology. If community is in apocalypse, patience, not grandiosity; attention, not dualism; earth, not escape, may see us through. Nothing is to be taken for granted. The gifts are not grants—they are yet always to be opened.

NOTES

1. For the best systematic treatment of these historical correlations, see Gerda Lerner, *The Creation of Patriarchy* (New York: Oxford University Press, 1986).

2. Elisabeth Schüssler Fiorenza's *In Memory of Her* shows the way in which canonization echoes the movement toward a hierarchical and assimilationist church, and therefore away from the egalitarian charismatic movement centered around Jesus as the eschatological prophet of Wisdom (New York: Crossroad, 1983).

3. For analysis of the sources of Western revolutions in the apocalyptic movements, cf. Norman Cohn, *The Pursuit of the Millennium* (New York: Oxford University Press, 1970 [originally published in 1961]); and Ernst Bloch, *The Principle of Hope* (Boston: MIT Press, 1986 [originally published in 1938–47]). Rosemary Radford Ruether comments in *Sexism and God Talk* on the implicit sexism of eschatological anthropologies, which defer full equality until the utopian or supernatural future ([Boston: Beacon Press, 1983], ch. 4). Yet the contemporary liberationist use of the Book of Revelation suggests the continued inadvisability of its dismissal by any progressive account of the cultural role of religion. See Alan Boesak, *Comfort and Protest: The Apocalypse from a South African Perspective* (Philadelphia: Westminster Press, 1987).

4. See Catherine Keller, "Women against Wasting the World: Notes on Ecology and Eschatology," in *Reweaving the World*, ed. Irene Diamond and Gloria Orenstein (San Francisco: Sierra Club Books, 1990).

5. Naylor tells stories of an embattled, dying neighborhood subject to the internalized pressures of poverty, racism, sexism, heterosexism— yet in which the redemptive moments take the shape of renewed communal connection.

6. Josiah Royce, *The Problem of Christianity*, vol. 1 (Chicago: Gateway Edition, 1968 [originally published in 1913]); pp. 392, 359.

7. Michel Foucault, *Power/Knowledge* (New York: Pantheon Books, 1980).

8. Sharon Welch, *Communities of Resistance and Solidarity* (Maryknoll, N.Y.: Orbis Books, 1986). See also her encouraging next step in the

theory of community, especially inspired by the dissident hope of African-American women writers to resist "cultured despair" (Sharon Welch, *A Feminist Ethic of Risk* [Minneapolis: Fortress Press, 1990]).

For an important contribution to communitarianism, see Herman Daly and John Cobb, *For the Common Good: Redirecting the Economy toward Community, the Environment, and a Sustainable Future* (Boston: Beacon Press, 1989). For a helpful warning against communitarianism, see Iris Marion Young, "The Ideal of Community and the Politics of Difference," in *Feminism/Postmodernism*, ed. Linda Nicholson (New York and London: Routledge & Kegan Paul, 1990).

12

Communities of Collaboration:
Shared Commitments/Common Tasks

GEORGE RUPP

THE TITLE ALREADY FORMULATES MY THESIS: without shared commitments or common tasks there can be no community. For sufficiently encompassing senses of "shared commitment," "common task," and "community," this thesis is no doubt noncontroversial — even self-evident. But it nonetheless invites attention precisely because of the changing character not only of community but also of commitment and work in modern pluralistic societies.

Beyond Blood and Soil

The prominence of the theme of community in contemporary literature and social commentary itself testifies to the deep sense of its lack at least in the consciousness of cultural elites in the modern West. This sense of absence or loss all too often indulges in not only nostalgia for an idealized past but also inattention to the continuing power of traditional communities. Both forms of indulgence should, of course, be resisted. But such resistance must not be allowed to obscure the contrast between large-scale, mobile, urban, and pluralistic societies on the one hand and small, settled, rural, and religiously and ethnically homogeneous communities on the other.

This contrast is so frequently evoked that it is difficult to avoid a barrage of platitudes and stereotypes. The bedrock virtues of the small town and country are corrupted in the big city. Mutual support and respect among individuals are supplanted by anonymous bureaucratic programs. Personal trust, shared responsibility, and cooperative effort surrender to impersonal market forces, and so on.

Academic discussion has dressed up the distinction in the jargon of *Gemeinschaft* and *Gesellschaft*. This distinction has become a fixture of social theory since its elaborate treatment in Ferdinand Tönnies's 1887 book entitled *Gemeinschaft und Gesellschaft*.[1] But the terms themselves also have a rich prior history in philosophical discussions and continuing currency as ordinary German words. To claim that all those uses are the same would be to over simplify egregiously. But each use of the distinction is identifying features also expressed in the platitudes and stereotypes. In short, intellectual reflection and popular wisdom agree in stressing a fundamental divide between traditional communities and modern bureaucratic societies.

To pose the contrast in those terms identifies the ends of a spectrum, which of course means that many communities both in the past and today illustrate points between the two extremes. But the bonds of community certainly assume different forms depending on where on the spectrum a society falls. Furthermore, because community is so often consciously or unconsciously construed as small, settled, rural, and homogeneous, it is sensed as lacking insofar as a society is large in scale, mobile, urban, and pluralistic.

This sense of deficiency correctly identifies the fact that for modern pluralistic societies, common bonds cannot simply be taken for granted. The implied contrast is also defensible: in more traditional communities, there are such taken-for-granted bonds because of close proximity over long periods of time. Mobility and anonymity first loosen and then often break ties that depend on genealogy and geography, on blood and soil. That such common bonds cannot be taken for granted does not in itself justify the conclusion that there is no sense of community in modern pluralistic societies. But in the modern world community is an achievement, not a given.

In modern Western societies, the loosening of natural bonds need not be belabored. When more and more people move frequently from one urban area to another, they do not have the investment, either personal or financial, in one particular place.

When work and leisure alike are widely dispersed, elaborate networks of acquaintances often replace direct contact with close friends and immediate neighbors. Similarly, impersonal bureaucracies and markets displace personal relationships as the media through which information is transmitted and products and services are distributed. Connections among members of even a nuclear family are strained because distance in both geography and culture is more the rule than the exception; and certainly members of extended families very rarely remain in close proximity to each other over multiple generations. In short, in the modern West the ties of blood are severely attenuated, the common ground of soil seriously eroded.

Outside the modern West, the bonds of blood and soil may continue to hold communities together more effectively. But the challenge to traditional ties is evident there as well. The threat to the traditional power of the extended family in postrevolutionary China is a graphic example. So is the tension between tribal affiliation and citizenship in postindependence Africa. Those issues are in significant part the result of intrusions from the West — for example, the impact of and resistance to Communism in China and the imposition on Africa of geographical divisions from the colonial era. But the result nonetheless remains a challenge to traditional patterns of small, stable, and homogeneous community.

India offers an especially arresting instance of such crosscurrents. In traditional India, the bonds of village and caste are strong indeed. But those bonds have been under sustained pressure in India from the colonial era on. The intellectual traditions, the legal patterns, and the commercial practices of the British empire have provided an alternative framework that does not depend directly on intra-Indian ethnic, linguistic, religious, or caste distinctions.

More crucial for postindependence India is the fact that indigenous leaders in turn have also resisted the centrifugal forces of ethnic, linguistic, religious, and caste differences. Even Gandhi, with his commitment to village life and simple technologies and his criticism of urbanization and industrialization, still insisted on a nation united under a secular constitution that precludes discrimination on the basis of religion or language or caste. This insistence became integral to the policies of postindependence India as Nehru led the country toward democratic socialism and a secularism that grounds legal rights on universal appeals to the human as such rather than on membership in one or another particular community.

As Leroy Rouner argues in his *To Be at Home: Christianity, Civil Religion, and Human Community*, Gandhi, Nehru, and their colleagues in the Indian independence movement drew on both Western and indigenous traditions to develop what in effect became a new and unified sense of identity for India, an identity that consciously attempts to incorporate traditional communities while also moving beyond their mutually exclusive and antagonistic claims.[2] This movement emphatically imbued its adherents with a sense of participation in a vital community. But, like Western societies, India today faces the continuing challenge of sustaining the power of such inclusive senses of community in a modern secular state that may have weakened though certainly has not entirely displaced more traditional loyalties.

The Ideal of Universal Community

The example of India is instructive in a double sense. It certainly illustrates the tensions between the claims of traditional communities and the requirements of large-scale societies. But the Indian case demonstrates as well that a movement convinced of its own historical significance may generate a powerful sense of shared identity among its participants.

This development is evident not only in the forging of national identities but also in transnational or universalizing movements that have shaped the modern world. The most striking instances of such movements are the great missionary religions — Buddhism, Christianity, and Islam — and their secular counterpart, Marxism. In each case, the goal of the movement is a finally universal community based on commitment or allegiance or solidarity rather than exclusively on natural bonds.

No doubt a crucial source of their power is the fact that such religions or secular movements may themselves be expressed or embodied in compelling and at least initially intimate communities. While such a movement may have a goal that is universal in scope, it also offers its members a sense of belonging to a community set over against the larger society. Indeed, just this attraction of membership in a community that is in principle inclusive can be crucial for the capacity of missionary religious movements to draw adherents from more established alternative traditions — as, for example, John Gager has argued in the case of early Christianity in his *Kingdom and Community*.[3]

But universalizing religious and secular movements are also implicated in the fate of the traditional communities they encounter. In some cases, missionary movements in effect become assimilated to the ties of blood and soil. The result is that missionary impulses become enmeshed in traditional mores. Think, for example, of the role of caste in predominantly Buddhist villages of Sri Lanka or of so-called animism in African Christianity. This result may be applauded as the legitimate and even unavoidable indigenization of a global tradition in a particular location or it may be attacked as uncritical acquiescence in established practices. Either way there is recognition of an assimilation of the missionary movement to the patterns of traditional communities.

In contrast to this tacit support of traditional communities are cases in which religious or secular movements are so intertwined with the origins and the structures of large-scale modern societies that they contribute at least indirectly to the undermining of traditional communities. The relationship of the Christian missionary movement to Western colonial rule in Asia, Africa, and Latin America not infrequently, perhaps even characteristically, illustrates this tendency. So, too, does the development of Marxism from a revolutionary movement to the officially established political credo of powerful modern states.

The conception of a community that is open and in intention inclusive has fundamentally shaped human sensibilities worldwide. It is affirmed and then presupposed not only in missionary religions like Buddhism, Christianity, and Islam and secular movements like Marxism but also in a host of other voluntary associations and international organizations. This ideal of inclusive community provides critical leverage over against both the provincialism of traditional communities and the complacency of established social order. As such, it is a crucial resource for all who recognize that a return to the intimacy and homogeneity and stability of traditional communities is not feasible but who also cannot wholeheartedly celebrate the domination of modern pluralistic societies by the impersonal processes of markets and bureaucracies.

Yet despite its power in shaping human sensibilities world-wide, this ideal of universal community frequently remains little more than an attractive abstraction. It may on occasion be embodied in intimate religious communities or in politically vital groups, usually for a brief period and on a small scale. The ideal of universal community may also become institutionalized in more established and longer-term forms. But in those forms it all too often fails to generate a sense of intimate and vital belonging even among those who affirm it ardently. Here international organizations promoting human welfare or voluntary associations dedicated to human rights face the same dilemma that confronts Christianity or Marxism. Pursuit of the ideal of universal community becomes so entangled with the market mechanisms and the bureaucratic processes of large scale modern societies that a sense of lively participation in a shared community is all but lost.

Certainly participation in particular institutional expressions of the ideal of universal community is to be affirmed, whether those institutional embodiments be small and cohesive groups or broader-based organizations — for example, a house church, a neighborhood housing co-op, Amnesty International, or UNICEF. Such groups and organizations are a crucial arena in which the struggle to realize community in modern societies is waged. Especially in view of the odds against that struggle, we should no doubt participate vigorously in the efforts of bodies or associations committed to representing the ideal of universal community. This participation cannot, however, by itself bear the full burden of our response to the challenge of realizing a sense of community in modern pluralistic societies.

Instead of placing this full burden on groups or organizations that are almost unavoidably marginal in the lives of most participants other than their full-time employees, we must assign a substantial share of the load to our central activities. For us as for our forebears, that means our love and our work. Few would question that our intimate personal relationships fundamentally shape our sense of participation in shared community — even if, or all the more because, those relationships are under great stress. In contrast, the centrality of work may be more disputable. The frustrations of often very routinized jobs together with shorter work weeks and substantial discretionary income mean that leisure activities play a significant role for increasing numbers of people. Yet important as love and leisure may be, they offer a precarious base for community if there is no sense of satisfaction from work.

From Vocation to Occupation

The centrality of work to our sense of participation in community is evident across an impressive range of times and places. Bands of hunters in tribal Africa join together in pursuing their common task. In traditional India, caste and occupation reflect and reinforce each other. In revolutionary China, work groups provide an important basis for collective identity. In contemporary Japan, a sense of belonging and mutual responsibility is imbued at various levels of corporate activity, from quite small quality circles to large firms as a whole.

This centrality of work to individual and corporate identity has a complex history in modern Western societies. Secular developments that often serve to undermine the foundations of traditional communities are themselves grounded in religious conceptions of vocation. We may not accept every point that Max Weber argues in *The Protestant Ethic and the Spirit of Capitalism.* But we can scarcely gainsay the impact of first the Lutheran and then even more the Calvinist insistence that worldly work no less than religious vocation is a divine calling.[4]

Modern Western societies have moved very far from the position of the Protestant reformers, albeit in the direction that they indicated. In its Reformation expressions, the dignifying of ordinary labor pointed to a way of imbuing work with such significance that it contributed to the sanctification of the world and the glorification of God. Celebration of the priesthood of all believers and interpretation of worldly work as a response to divine calling engendered disciplined activity and careful calibration of achievements as signs of God's grace. Over time this inner-worldly asceticism, to use Weber's term, was, however, increasingly severed from its religious roots. Disciplined activity and careful calibration of achievements certainly continued. But the long-term effect was to advance and to legitimate the thorough secularization of economic life.

This thorough secularization of economic life is at the core of the development of those institutional forms that distinguish modern societies from traditional communities: in a word, *Gesellschaft* displaces *Gemeinschaft*. In such simplified polar contrasts, there undeniably lurks the danger of nostalgia for an idealized and in any case irretrievable sense of intimate community, a nostalgia expressed in both reactionary and utopian forms. Yet despite that danger, the contrasts do register an accurate measure of critical deficiencies in the understanding of work in modern secular societies.

The total reduction of ends to means or at least the complete domination of ends by means extracts human action from contexts of meaning that afford a sense of accomplishment and satisfaction larger than the one entailed in the discrete acts themselves. To testify with the Protestant reformers that work contributes to the sanctification of the world and the glorification of God may sound archaic or quaint. But the sense of connection to which this testimony bears witness is nonetheless sorely needed when work too often no longer points beyond itself to more inclusive purposes that it participates in realizing; when, in short, work is reduced from vocation to occupation.

Not only in *The Protestant Ethic and the Spirit of Capitalism* but also in his influential writings on bureaucracy and other characteristic features of modern secular societies, Max Weber brooded over this set of issues. Weber's thought provides a point of orientation for continuing discussions. Jürgen Habermas summarizes the transition from traditional communities to modern societies. Habermas refers as well to more recent thinkers, but in the end he develops his own position by reformulating the central Weberian concept of rationalization.

Habermas notes that in traditional communities, economic activities presuppose a normative sociocultural framework and are conducted within the limits of that framework. This framework is grounded in unquestioned mythical, religious, or metaphysical interpretations of reality that provide legitimation for economic and other subsystems of action. In short, a community is defined as traditional insofar as a normative sociocultural framework is superordinate to instrumental action in its various forms. In contrast, societies are more modern than traditional insofar as instrumental action extends its reach beyond previously established lim-

its, calls into question traditional forms of authority, and in effect
provides legitimation through its own productive power. The logical extreme of this development is "a fundamental reversal" in that
a normative sociocultural framework no longer sets limits for all
forms of instrumental action but is instead completely absorbed
into them.[5]

Habermas affirms the reorganization of social institutions
through the extension of subsystems of instrumental actions and
the attendant questioning of traditional authorities. To describe
this process, he adopts Weber's term, "rationalization." But he also
uses this concept in a second sense, namely, what he calls "rationalization at the level of the institutional framework." Even as he
acknowledges the extension of subsystems of instrumental action,
he at the same time calls for the reestablishment of a public context or framework for that action.[6]

Habermas develops this line of reasoning in direct continuity
with Weber's thought. He explicitly refers in particular to Weber's
analysis of *zweckrationale Aktion*, which I have rendered simply
as "instrumental action" (rather than using a more literal but also
quite cumbersome translation—"purposive-rational action," for
example). Habermas presents his reformulation as going beyond
what he characterizes as Weber's subjective approach. But Habermas's description of the extension of subsystems of instrumental
or purposive-rational action is clearly an adaptation of Weber's
concept of rationalization.

Less explicitly continuous with Weber's thought is the second sense in which Habermas uses the concept of rationalization,
namely, at the sociocultural or normative level. The continuity is
significant because it reinforces the shared resistance of Habermas and Weber to nostalgic idealizations of *Gemeinschaft* over
against *Gesellschaft*. Weber's distinction between *Zweckrationalität*
(purposive or instrumental rationality) and *Wertrationalität* (value
or normative rationality) is well known and often invoked. Less
well known is his correlation of this distinction with the contrast
between *Gemeinschaft* and *Gesellschaft*—or better, to use Weber's
preferred terms, *Vergemeinschaftung* and *Vergesellschaftung* (verbal nouns perhaps less susceptible to reification than Tönnies's
simpler substantives). The conception of *Wertrationalität* may all
too easily be invoked as representative of the traditional norma-

tive framework that the *Zweckrationalität* of modernity undermines. That appeal would contrast with Habermas's focus on the need to reestablish a normative context or framework, albeit one that does not repudiate the extension of subsystems of instrumental action that characterizes modernity. Any appeal to *Wertrationalität* that aligns it simply with traditional communities over against modern society is, however, also at odds with Weber's own analysis.

In the opening sections of *Economy and Society*, the magnum opus left uncompleted at his death, Weber outlines a taxonomy of types of social action. He specifies four such types: instrumentally rational (*zweckrational*); value-rational (*wertrational*); affectual; and traditional.[7] This typology in turn structures the categorical scheme he develops to systematize such other issues as types of order or bases of legitimacy. Significant in regard to the question of a normative framework for posttraditional societies is that he identifies not only instrumentally rational but also value-rational action with *Vergesellschaftung* rather than with *Vergemeinschaftung*.[8]

Weber notes his debt to Tönnies, but he develops the distinction so as to emphasize more clearly than Tönnies did that communality (*Vergemeinschaftung*) and association (*Vergesellschaftung*) refer to ideal types. He also observes that from the point of view of instrumentally rational action, value-rational action always appears to be irrational. Yet he nonetheless insists that value-rational action is a type of orientation that continues to be crucial in modern secular society — indeed, so much so that "orientation of action wholly to the rational achievement of ends without relation to fundamental values is . . . essentially only a limiting case."[9]

This excursus into the formulations of Habermas and Weber serves to sharpen the question. Work is virtually by definition instrumental action. Indeed, in distinguishing purposive-rational action from the normative institutional framework that he argues it presupposes and requires, Habermas uses the shorthand contrast of "work" and "interaction."[10] While this reduction of work to instrumental action oversimplifies, it nonetheless indicates how far secular attitudes toward work are from the conception of vocation. But beyond this confirmation that for most members of modern secular societies the transition from vocation to occupation has long since been completed, the fact that work so clearly and centrally exemplifies instrumental action makes it an especially apt test case of whether and how such action may still point beyond itself to more inclusive purposes that it participates in realizing.

Shared Commitments/Common Tasks

While work exemplifies instrumental action, it also offers distinctive strengths for addressing the question of community in contemporary pluralistic societies. Shared commitment through common tasks does not depend on particular ethnic or geographical qualifications. The sense of community that may eventuate from such shared commitments accordingly is not restricted to the bonds of traditional communities. At the same time, the sense of community resulting from involvement in common tasks may be central to particular, concrete, mundane actualities in ways that movements devoted to the ideal of universal community all too often are not. Thus the sense of community associated with work may be especially well suited to modern pluralistic societies because it is particular or concrete, central to secular life, and yet also in principle nonexclusive.

Habermas wants a repoliticized decision making to prevent the complete absorption of all normative considerations into subsystems of instrumental action. But his appeal to unrestricted discussion, to undistorted communication, is in danger of being disconnected from those subsystems of instrumental action. Here Weber's sober insistence on integral relations between abstract ideals and concrete patterns of action is salutary. This emphasis is sharply expressed in his two late lectures on vocation. In "Politics as a Vocation," he is dismissive of those who indulge in "mystic flight from reality" because "they have not measured up to the world as it really is in its everyday routine." Similarly, in "Science [*Wissenschaft*] as a Vocation," he insists that even the most exalted work must meet "the demands of the day." In perhaps his most vivid image, he describes politics and in doing so allows it to exemplify every vocation: it is "a strong and slow boring of hard boards."[11]

It is easy enough to conjure up examples that register this point, albeit in ways that trade in stereotypes perhaps more characteristic of the past than of the future: the utterly routinized labor of bored assembly line workers in a manufacturing plant or of immigrant seamstresses in a sweatshop or of salesclerks meeting their quotas in a discount store or of brokers pushing their investments over the phone. This routinization of labor is, of course, also evident in institutional settings that have quite explicit larger purposes. Hospitals may have many workers who execute routinized tasks that they themselves deem to be only very remotely connected to medical care or healing. This number may count clerical staff who process forms, custodians who keep floors clean, technicians who repair equipment. But it also may include health professionals whose assignments have become so specialized or so focused on technical proficiency or so preoccupied with efficiency that they sense little connection to the process of medical care or healing. So, too, in schools or in law offices the work not only of clerical, custodial, and technical staff but also of professionals may have become so absorbed into bureaucratic and market-oriented subsystems of action that any larger purposes recede to the periphery of awareness. An institution may have more exalted general goals. But the pressing need to execute specific tasks is measured against very mundane standards that do not take those larger general goals into direct account.

This situation, which we cannot but recognize as characteristic of virtually all large-scale institutions in our society, demands responses on at least two levels. First, we must ask whether and how even in such large-scale institutional settings we may still attain a sense of community through an awareness of shared commitment to common tasks. Second, we must assess the relative adequacy of the commitments and tasks that may foster this sense of community. The space limitations for this paper do not allow a detailed response on either level. In each case I will, however, sketch an approach that I find promising; and in doing so I will at the same time attempt to draw together the several lines of argument I have developed.

In his *Tales of a New America*, Robert Reich formulates a conception that provides a helpful point of reference for this drawing together of the several lines of argument I have developed.

Much of the political debate over economic policy tacitly or otherwise presupposed the existence of these two categories of activity: entrepreneurial and drone. In the popular mind, people were not fated for one or the other category; the distinction had nothing to do with class. Almost anyone could become an entrepreneur, with enough drive and daring. The economy needed both, of course — creative entrepreneurs to formulate the Big Ideas that would find their way into new products and production techniques, and drones to undertake the routine chores involved in realizing these ideas. But for the economy to prosper, it was presumed necessary to reward people who opted to become entrepreneurs and discipline those who remained drones.[12]

Over against this characterization, Reich presents a quite different orientation that he argues is more adequate for meeting the demands of the new global economy in which we unavoidably participate: "Instead of a handful of lone entrepreneurs producing a few industry-making Big Ideas, innovation must be more continuous and collective."[13] Enterprises designed to reduce costs through mass production are organized in a series of hierarchical tiers, so that each superior can ensure that subordinates are working according to plan. In contrast, "collective entrepreneurialism" requires a relatively flat structure in which incremental advances are continuously discovered and applied so as to improve products and processes. Furthermore, because tasks are often so intertwined, success can be measured only in reference to the collective results of work groups or teams.[14]

Reich draws many of his analogies and illustrations from Japanese firms. But he acknowledges other instances of collective entrepreneurialism. America, for example, now provides both "professional partnerships" and "small firms producing service-intensive goods." Professional partnerships include associations of lawyers, doctors, accountants, management consultants, architects, or even investment bankers in which the value of the enterprise is almost exclusively a function of the knowledge and experience of its members. Similarly, in small firms producing service-intensive goods, experts in design, fabrication, and marketing form coalitions that

involve few established routines and little hierarchy as all participants contribute to a common enterprise.[15]

Reich's conception of collective entrepreneurialism indicates
an approach to attaining a sense of community even in contexts
dominated by the impersonal processes of markets and bureaucracies. Within large-scale institutions, groups or teams of colleagues may express shared commitments and identify with each
other in executing common tasks. Members of such groups or teams
need not and typically will not be related by family ties or geographical origins. Instead they will collaborate on the basis of competencies that complement each other and are required for the
task at hand. An example is what at least optimally would be the
collaboration of doctors, nurses, technicians, clerical staff, the patient, and his or her family in the setting of the hospital operating
room and its supporting facilities. Other instances include a research team in a university laboratory or a product development
group in a corporation or a rescue squad responding to emergency
calls or a construction team specializing in building rehabilita-
tion or an investment banking group dealing in mergers and ac-
quisitions or a sabotage strike force operating in hostile territory
or an organizing committee for a series of protest demonstrations.

The challenge we face is to extend the contexts in which this
sense of community through collaboration is attained. In this respect, less hierarchical organizational structures that value initiative and shared responsibility at all levels are surely a step in the
right direction. So too is the sustained effort to include a range
of competencies and orientations in the group of collaborators.
In the case of medical care, for example, the team will be more
effective if and insofar as it comes to include not only doctors and
nurses of diverse specialties, but also medical technicians, clerical
and other staff, and, very importantly, the patient and his or her
family as well. Similarly, in the life of our colleges and universities, the relatively flat organizational structure that we dignify
as shared governance in many ways offers a model for other more
hierarchical organizations in our society. Accordingly, this commitment to collegiality and shared responsibility must be preserved
and strengthened. At the same time, though, members of college
and university communities in addition to faculty must be incor-

porated with greater sensitivity and recognition into the team of collaborators.

Insofar as our work exemplifies such collaboration, it may provide a sense not only of individual identity but also of participation in community that is the more crucial insofar as a society is dominated by impersonal markets and bureaucracies. This sense of participation in community through one's work certainly does not replace or render superfluous memberships in voluntary associations of all kinds. It does, however, offer the prospect of expressing shared commitments in and through common tasks that are central to daily activities even within large-scale contemporary institutions.

This prospect raises my second and final question, namely, the relative adequacy of the commitments and tasks that may indeed foster such a sense of community. This further question follows unavoidably from the fact that not every shared commitment or common task is to be affirmed simply because it contributes to realizing a sense of community. The *esprit de corps* of Nazi storm troopers and the potent bonds of solidarity in crime families register this point sharply. But less melodramatic illustrations of the issue also demand attention: the task force formed to defeat a hostile corporate takeover bid, whose members become so engrossed in the intensity of the competition and the scale of the stakes that they bend legal restraints or ignore the legitimate interests of shareholders or other employees of the firm; the research group so intent not only on discovery but also on recognition that it cooks laboratory data or fails to acknowledge contributions of other researchers or expends funds without authorization; the collegiate football team that conspires to, or at least connives in, circumventing regulations on academic requirements or drug use.

This evident fact that not every shared commitment or common task is to be affirmed just because it contributes to a sense of community invites and perhaps even requires a renewed appreciation of the critical power of the ideal of universal community. Even as we celebrate the sense of community that shared commitment to a common task may foster, we must also affirm the ideal of community that is respectful toward the whole of reality and therefore also to all members of the human community because it is in principle universal rather than limited by ethnic or geographical qualification. In short, while we seek to counter the patterns of modern secular *Gesellschaft* that inhibit a sense of community, we must also resist the provincial exclusivism of *Gemeinschaft*. Only this double vigilance will allow a celebration of community that does not risk degenerating into collective self-glorification. Put positively, this double vigilance allows the affirmation of a sense of community that is viable in contemporary pluralistic societies.

NOTES

1. Ferdinand Tönnies, *Community and Society (Gemeinschaft und Gesellschaft)*, ed. and trans. Charles P. Loomis (East Lansing: Michigan State University Press, 1957).

2. Leroy S. Rouner, *To Be at Home: Christianity, Civil Religion, and Human Community* (Boston: Beacon Press, 1991).

3. John G. Gager, *Kingdom and Community: The Social World of Early Christianity* (Englewood Cliffs, N.J.: Prentice-Hall, 1975).

4. Max Weber, *The Protestant Ethic and the Spirit of Capitalism*, trans. Talcott Parsons (New York: Charles Scribner's Sons, 1958), esp. pp. 79–128.

5. Jürgen Habermas, *Toward a Rational Society: Student Protest, Science, and Politics*, trans. Jeremy J. Shapiro (Boston: Beacon Press, 1970), esp. pp. 94–107.

6. Ibid., pp. 118–20.

7. Max Weber, *Economy and Society: An Outline of Interpretive Sociology*, ed. Guenther Roth and Claus Wittich (New York: Bedminster Press, 1968), vol. 1, pp. 24–26. Since so much of the interpretation turns on verbal distinctions that have no common English counterparts, compare *Wirtschaft und Gesellschaft: Grundriss der verstehenden Soziologie*, ed. Johannes Winckelmann (Tübingen: J.C.B. Mohr-Paul Siebeck, 1956), pp. 12–13.

8. Weber, *Economy and Society*, vol. 1, pp. 40–43; *Wirtschaft und Gesellschaft*, pp. 21–23.

9. Weber, *Economy and Society*, vol. 1, p. 26; *Wirtschaft und Gesellschaft*, p. 13. A less expansive rendering of Weber's admittedly very terse statement is "Absolute instrumental rationality of action is, however, also only in essence a heuristic (*konstuktiver*) limiting case."

10. Habermas, *Toward a Rational Society*, esp. pp. 91–94.

11. *From Max Weber: Essays in Sociology*, trans. H. H. Gerth and

C. Wright Mills (New York: Oxford University Press, Galaxy Books), pp. 128, 156.

    12. Robert B. Reich, *Tales of a New America: The Anxious Liberal's Guide to the Future* (New York: Random House, Vintage Books, 1987), p. 109.

    13. Ibid., p. 121.

    14. Ibid., pp. 125–26.

    15. Ibid., pp. 126–27.

Author Index

Subject Index

Africa, 2, 107, 109, 194, 196, 198
amazement, 174, 176
American society, 130, 142–43
apocalypse, 177–90
art, 3–4, 27–53, 160
atheists, 57, 167
autonomy, 1, 2, 3, 4, 6, 11, 23, 28, 32–33, 48, 95, 119

Buddhism, 82, 138, 153, 155, 195–96

caste, 8, 76, 87, 135, 194, 196
ceremonies, 15–17
China, 2, 7–8, 16, 81, 117–28, 194, 198
Christianity, 58, 78, 150, 153, 155–57, 160, 168, 173, 178–79, 181–82, 186–87, 195–97
coercive power, 2, 17–18
communes, 1, 122, 184
Communism, 1, 194
conformity, 6, 98, 104
Confucianism, 120–21, 123–27
cosmos, 119–20, 125
creative anarchy, 3, 5, 8, 24–25
creative power, 2–3, 17–18

democracy, 1, 9, 150–54, 160, 195
determinism, 4, 35–38, 41
diversity, 9–10, 92, 103, 150–60, 163, 169–74
dualism, 5, 81, 86

emotion, 46
environmental issues, 39, 42, 133, 152–53, 156, 158–59, 166, 180, 182
equality, 8, 121, 130, 167, 179, 180, 185

family, 24, 93–95, 97, 100, 111, 120–21, 123–28, 177, 181, 194
feminism, 10, 19, 153–54, 177–90
friendship, 121, 165, 171, 180, 183

Gemeinschaft, 7, 117, 119–21, 123, 128, 150, 193, 199–200, 207
Germany, 1
Gesellschaft, 7, 117, 120, 122–25, 126–28, 150, 193, 199–200, 207
God, 1, 4–5, 10, 29, 49–52, 57, 61–62, 66–68, 73, 78, 82, 85–87, 115, 120, 122, 138, 143, 150, 157, 159, 163–64, 166–68, 170, 172–73, 175–76, 180, 182, 185–86, 198

harmony, 95–96, 99
Hinduism, 134–37, 143, 177–78
hope, 183–85, 188–89

imagination, 27, 48, 159
incommensurability, 57, 61–64, 73
India, 2, 11, 16, 141, 194–95

211